Will The Real Holy Ghost Please Stand Up

A Book of Witness

by

Angela Powell

Edited by: Sistah Debra Bonaparte of Atlanta, Georgia

Copyright © 2015 by Angela Powell

All rights reserved; except for images taken from Wikipedia and Microsoft Clipart

Library of Congress Cataloging-in-Publication Data

ISBN-10: 1517631211

ISBN-13: 978-1517631215

Winter So(-u)ls-tice Action Date: Tuesday, 22 December 2015, at 04:49

Alpha Khen Omega Publications, McDonough, Georgia, USA

1. Religion – Psychology of Religion. 2. Egypt Spirituality – Pharaoh Akhenaton. 3. Educational – Egyptian, Greek, Hebrew Etymology.

Available Titles:

1. Spiritual Bipolar: God Is The Peace In Your Heart That Calms The Voices Above Your Head
2. 10 Plagues Placed On Egypt: Murdering Our Godhead
3. Will The Real Holy Ghost Please Stand Up
4. Jehovah's and Abraham's 3-Fold Curse of Captivity Against The Black Man

Upcoming Titles In This Series, Available Soon:

5. Abraham, Isaac, and Jacob: Holy Patriarchs or Evil Sorcerers from Ur of the Chaldees?
6. Caesar's Dollar: Mark of the Beast

Bible verses taken from James the king of England Authorized Version (kjv).

 Make Sure To Cross Reference With **TEN PLAGUES PLACED ON EGYPT: MURDERING OUR GODHEAD**

This book is dedicated to you, heirs of Shem and his brother, Japheth the elder, because even though this is The Second Coming and a new beginning for the Redeemed, the time of your end has come. Gird yourselves for the War of Gog and Magog with your Father-- the Devil, and go down with him and burn in the lake of fire with him…because you know the truth and still refuse to repent for enslaving the holy seed; and you refuse to convert to The Aten, know that He is the Sun of righteousness with healing in His wings, Who cures the White Supremacy Illness.

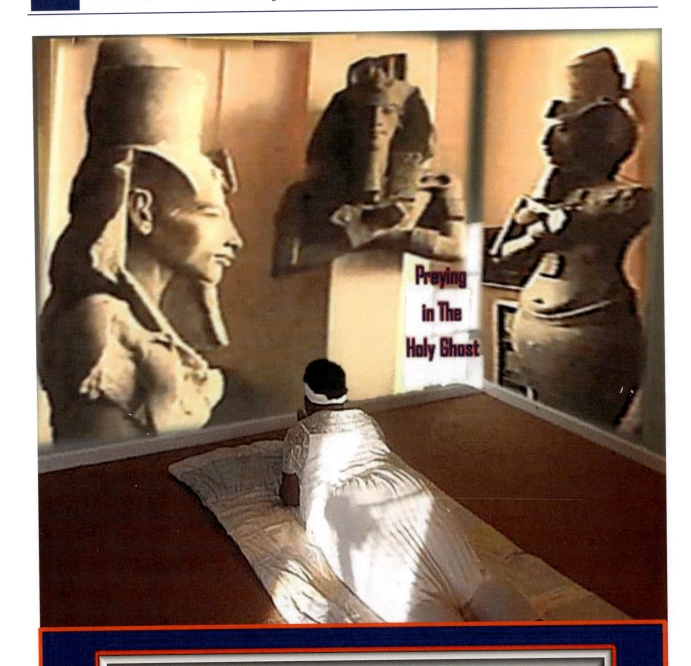

The Lord God Alpha Khen Omega, as dictated to Angela Powell

John 14:16 – 20

And I will pray the Father, and he shall give you another Comforter, that he may abide with you for ever; Even the Spirit of truth; whom the world cannot receive, because it seeth him not, neither knoweth him: but ye know him; for he dwelleth with you, and shall be in you.

I will not leave you comfortless: I will come to you. Yet a little while, and the world seeth me no more; but ye see me: because I live, ye shall live also. At that day ye shall know that I am in my Father, and ye in me, and I in you (John 14:16-20).

Moving Beyond *Reading In Tongues* and Translating To Speaking With Your Two-Edged Sword

Revelation 1:16 (kjv authorized)

And he had in his right hand seven stars: and out of his mouth went a **sharp twoedged sword**: and his countenance was as the sun shineth in his strength.

Revelation 1:16 (Translated)

And he had in his right hand seven stars: and out of his mouth went *just-now-words with power to scatter the enemy*: and his countenance was as *The Aten* shineth in his strength.

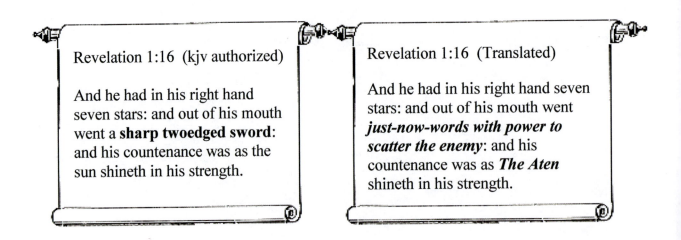

The Lord God Alpha Khen Omega, as dictated to Angela Powell

Contents

Moving Beyond Reading In Tongues and Translating To Speaking With Your Two-Edged Sword 6
- Ankh Key: Unlocking Doors Of Your Mind 8
- The Power of Writing Down My Thoughts (Test Yourself Journaling Page) 9
- Introducing The Aten, The Lord God Alpha Khen Omega 11
- The Pictographic Conclusion of The Matter 13
- A Redeemed Captive's Log 15
- "THESE BE TALISMANS" 18
- A Redeemed Captive's Log 19
- Question: Portray of The Holy Ghost as a White Dove, Truth or fiction 21
- I Am Come To Reverse The Curse of The 10 Plagues Placed On Egypt 22

WORD STUDY: 25
- Falcon/Dove that Remains on Pharaoh Khafre 31
- Dove/Falcon = Vulture = To See 34
- A Parable: Eye of Rā + Vulture 35
- Solution: Eye of Rā + Vulture 36
- Dove = Falcon = Vulture = (Ra'ah) To See 36
- The Aten Speaks: Team Atenites…Ready. Set. GO! 37
- Instructions for Interpreting "The Virgin Birth" Parable 38
- Biblical References: Revelation 1:16 – RIGHT NOW Words 39
- MESSAGE IN HEBRAIC TONGUE 40
- Sociolinguists' Biblical Slant On The Egyptian Nativity 42
- Matthew 1:18, Opening A Mystery About The Nativity 45
- The Power Of Writing Down My Thoughts: Test Yourself Journaling Page 47
- Arise From Your Comfort Zone: Change Your Perspective: Break The Spell of Curse #1 49
- **Message In The Hamitic Tongue:** The Aten Speaks On True Deliverer 52
- The Power of Writing Down My Thoughts: Test Yourself Journaling Page 55
- Nativity Chart 57
- The Aten Speaks On The Kerygma of Lod: 58
- The Aten Speaks: Answering Rachel 62
- Changing Lanes from Shem and Japheth over to Ham 65
- Daily News: 22 December 2015, 04:49 am 69
- ~~~~BEGIN INTERPRETATION~~~~Two-Edged Sword 70
- The Power of Writing Down My Thoughts (Test Yourself Journaling Page) 77

WORD STUDY: Christ = Impassable Interval = Winter Solstice 2015 86
- Impassable Interval Concluding Message 86
- Change Your Perspective: Rise and Convert 87
- Revelation 11:19, The Temple of The Aten is Opened 88
- This is You! You Are A Spiritual Person Under Amen Covenant of Life 90
- Revelation 15:1-5, Standing On The Sea of Glass With Victory 93
- Instructions for Winter Solstice 2015 95
- Solution to the Pictographic Conclusion 96
- King Tutankhamen's War Trumphets To Be Sounded During Winter Solstice 97
- How To Use The Strong's Hebrew/Greek Concordance on CD-ROM 104
- Jehovah = God of mischief 108
- Answer Key 109

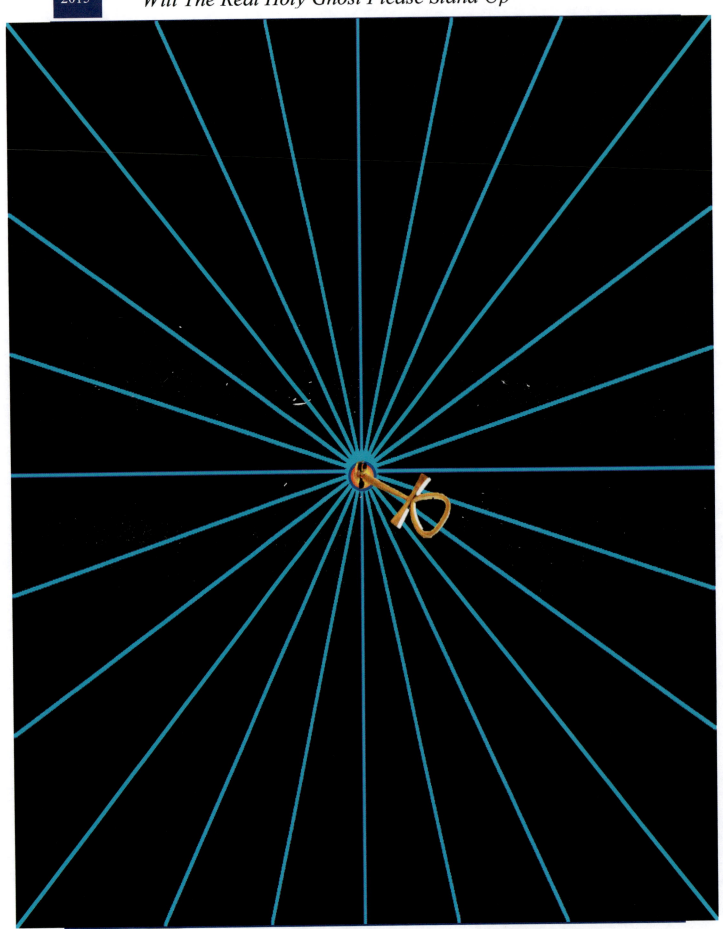

Make Sure To Cross Reference With TEN PLAGUES PLACED ON EGYPT: MURDERING OUR GODHEAD

The Power of Writing Down My Thoughts (Test Yourself Journaling Page)

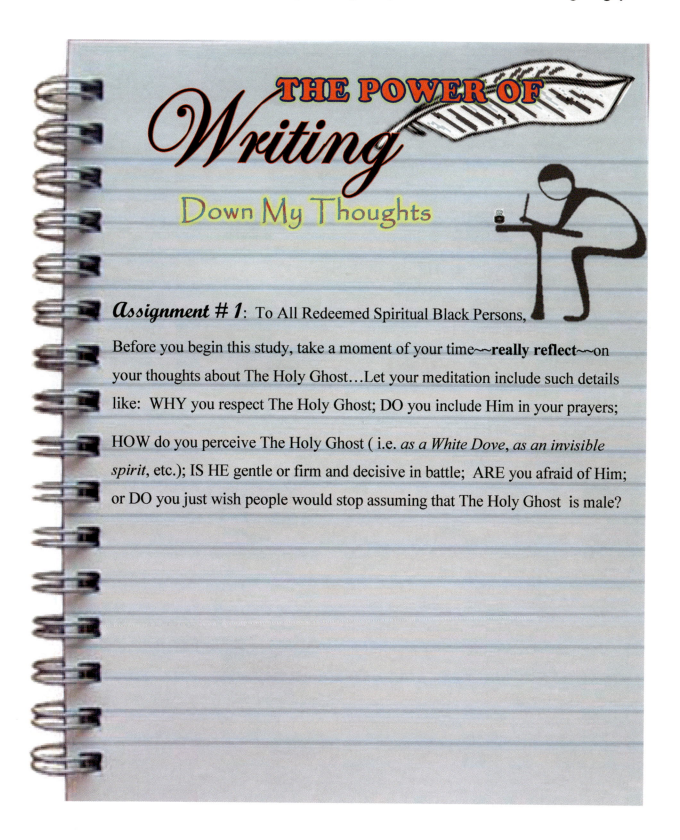

THE POWER OF Writing Down My Thoughts

Assignment #1: To All Redeemed Spiritual Black Persons,

Before you begin this study, take a moment of your time~~**really reflect**~~on your thoughts about The Holy Ghost…Let your meditation include such details like: WHY you respect The Holy Ghost; DO you include Him in your prayers;

HOW do you perceive The Holy Ghost (i.e. *as a White Dove*, *as an invisible spirit*, etc.); IS HE gentle or firm and decisive in battle; ARE you afraid of Him; or DO you just wish people would stop assuming that The Holy Ghost is male?

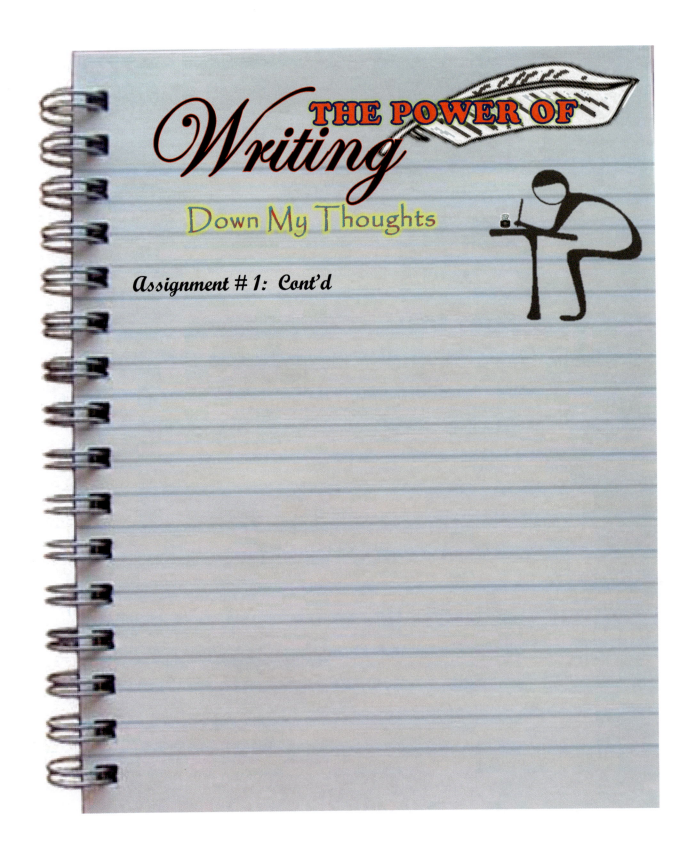

The Lord God Alpha Khen Omega, as dictated to Angela Powell

I Am Pharaoh Akhenaton. My reign was circa BC 1375-1350. The exact timeframe of the Exodus is unknown; but it is taught that the Exodus occurred during My rule; therefore, using My servant, Angela, I Am here to tell you exactly what happened!

On various pages, I will jot down a few facts that I want you to keep in mind:

FACT 1

Pharaoh comes from the title "Sa Ra," which means "Son of God."

FACT 2

It is taught of the Egyptians that we worshipped many Gods. During My rule, there was only One God, Re-Harakhti-in-his-name-Shu-who is Aten.

I Am The Aten.

(Matthew 11:27)

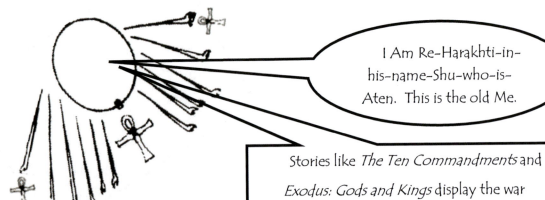

The Lord God Alpha Khen Omega, as dictated to Angela Powell

A word fitly spoken is like apples of gold in pictures of silver (Proverbs 25:11).

The Pictographic Conclusion of the Matter

Dove (The Holy Ghost) = Jonah (The Destroyer)

Falcon (subset) Vulture (subset) To See/Perceive/Understand (then) Make a burning

A Redeemed Captive's Log

Captive's Log

On 25 April 2012, or thereabout, I published a memoir titled, SPIRITUAL BIPOLAR: GOD IS THE PEACE IN YOUR HEART THAT CALMS THE VOICES ABOVE YOUR HEAD.

It is a Book of Witness for God, testifying to the facts surrounding why Black people were, are, and possibly shall be *again*, enslaved.

The Lord our God began to teach me these life-and-spirit-altering lessons in March 1994. At some point during my journey, I began to hear voices…and…well, you can learn about the rest of the story when you read the book.

But there is one experience I must share with you RIGHT NOW.

It is written on pages 109 – 111 of Spiritual Bipolar.

Here is a little summary:

One of the voices blasphemed The Holy Ghost with such vehemence that I would literally take to my bed and become depressed, afraid, feel defeated, and succumb to mental illness. After a year of this hostile **telepathic intrusion**, on a particular day, I found the courage to defeat the impious cursing coming from the voice above my head.

Read how I describe it in the Book of Witness:

Captive's Log

Excerpt from SPIRITUAL BIPOLAR: God Is The Peace In Your Heart That Calms The Voices Above Your Head

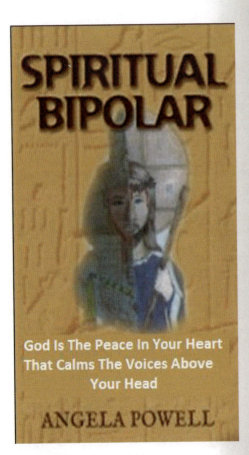

Pages 109 - 111

Chapter 17

"These Be Talismans," Thus Said The Lord

October 1999

"I can hear you," I spoke inside the privacy of my mind. Lips tightly zipped and unmovable, I continued to address those Spirits that only I could hear. "Those are your words, your blasphemy, not mine," I said.

I could hear one of their voices above my head. Its belligerent words pierced my soul, trying to kill my Spirit like poisonous darts thrown at an unclad man of little faith. Since 1994, this vicious voice blasphemed The Holy Ghost inside my head. It was not a little bitty voice. A peep or whisper, it was not. It was loud and threatening and defiant and even though I couldn't see it, I thought it was like a giant—an invisible giant—like the Philistine champion that David, the king of Israel, slew with stones, then cut off his head.

No stones were in my hand. Sin was in my life. I had no helmet of salvation, no vestures of righteousness, no shield of faith as Saul-Paul of Tarsus (whom God

The Lord God Alpha Khen Omega, as dictated to Angela Powell

Excerpt from SPIRITUAL BIPOLAR: God Is The Peace In Your Heart That Calms The Voices Above Your Head

had manifested as the false-Prophet) wrote in his epistle. I couldn't slay Spirits. I couldn't slay Saul-Paul. I had no way of fighting against principalities, against powers and rulers of darkness that my fellow earthlings upheld as the light of this world. Yet, I'd had enough of the voice. I couldn't take it "no mo'e."

Conjuring the bravery of *The Last Unicorn,* I stopped crying long enough to inch my head from underneath my comforter.

"I don't know who you are," my mind chastened the Spirit. "I don't know what you want from me but I will never let the blasphemous cursing you shout above my head travel out of my lips. Never! You can torture me for the rest of my life but I won't allow your curses to escape from between my lips! And I won't think it because **it's not** my thought! It's you—not me! I can't make you go away but I'm done crying and being scared of you!"

Once I launched a counterattack, like the parting of the Red Sea, the eerie shadows of a dozen combative Principalities departed from the dark realms that overshadowed my home. I felt a lifting of burdens as their darkness dissipated, and I knew those forces, those powers that be, those wicked Spirits in high places could no longer hinder my prayers.

I kneeled before The Lord and confessed I could discern reality from mythology and that I had learned to discern fables and deceptions from the real truth. All most all the ancient religions had stories of its God's virgin birth, death by crucifixion, and divine resurrection. It was a shocking revelation, one that, even though I had studied world mythology, I couldn't readily recall. The discovery blew my mind!

As Christians, we are taught that Jesus Christ is the only one who was born of a virgin, died by crucifixion, and resurrected to save the world from sin. Well, he wasn't. All the religious Gods, on the adjacent page, have the same story as Christ, and they were written thousands of years before Christ. What, then, is the origin of the Savior's story?

Egypt!

The first Savior's story is documented on pyramid walls.

Clothed in my right mind (meaning I'd discovered the Savior's origins), I prayed about the voices I'd been hearing, confessing that I did not know what it is or who it is but that it was telepathy and it was evil.

I confessed to God that He dwells within us and communes with us through The Holy Ghost.

Communion is good.

Telepathy is evil.

After my prayer, in a night vision, God showed me the busts of men and said, "These be talismans."

(End....pages 109 -111 of Spiritual Bipolar)

"THESE BE TALISMANS."

FIGHTING AGAINST TALISMANS, AGAINST PRINCIPALITIES, AGAINST POWERS, AGAINST THE RULERS OF THE DARKNESS OF THIS WORLD, AGAINST SPIRITUAL WICKEDNESS IN HIGH PLACES.

NAMES OF THE DEVIL
Egyptian = Amen, the Devil, Set, Apophis, Aapep, Saatt ta
Hebrew = Jehovah, Adversary, Satan, Serpent
       the satans, the antichrists
Phoenician = Baal
Greek = Zeus
Roman = Jupiter
Latin = Jove, Providence

2000 – 1800 BC ?

1750 BC ?

1500 - 1000 BC?

750 - 500 BC ?

551 BC ?

560 BC

AD 325
1st Council of Nicaea

AD 570

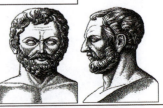

"THESE BE TALISMAN"

Make Sure To Cross Reference With **TEN PLAGUES PLACED ON EGYPT: MURDERING OUR GODHEAD**

A Redeemed Captive's Log

Captive's Log

The Lord our God gave me the Victory over the Beast and his Evil Spirit, on that day.

RIGHT NOW, however, this research and journaling bring back my anguish because in my search for truth, I have to be extra careful not to blaspheme The Holy Ghost. I still feel fear when broaching the subject because God's stern judgement "NO FORGIVENESS" is ever present with me.

Matthew 12:1-37; Mark 3:28-30; and Luke 12:10 state the only sin that will damn your soul is the blasphemy of The Holy Ghost. Yet, it is The Lord our God Who calls not only me; but you, too, to investigate the meanings of the words "holy" and "ghost."

It is reported that the Catholic Douay Rheims says "Holy Ghost" 95 while it uses "Holy Spirit" a total of 8 times.

My Sword Searchers kjv Bible uses "Holy Ghost" 89 times, found only in the New Testament. It uses "Holy Spirit" a mere 7 times: Three times in the Old Testament and four times in the New Testament. No other Bibles use the title "Holy Ghost." They all opt for "Holy Spirit."

Perhaps there is nothing wrong with that. I am sensitive to the title "Holy Ghost" because I grew up under elders who faithfully called upon The Holy Ghost. Therefore, that is the Title I shall use for this study.

With that in mind, using *Strong's Hebrew and Greek Concordance* on CD-Rom; *The Hieroglyphic Dictionary, Vol. I and II, 1978;* and "Pokorny Etymology of the Indo-European Roots" which is affixed to the *American Heritage Dictionary (AHD)*, 1968; **let us solve the**

Captive's Log

mystery of the pictograph and uncover a hidden truth about The Holy Ghost.

We are not alone--The Spirit of The Lord our God is RIGHT NOW helping us to arrive at His Truth.

To learn the procedures for using these reference books, refer to God's Book of Witness titled TEN PLAGUES PLACED ON EGYPT: MURDERING OUR GODHEAD.

Here are the results:

Holy

+

Ghost

The Lord God Alpha Khen Omega, as dictated to Angela Powell

Questions:

Is The Portrayal of "The Holy Ghost" as a "White Dove," Truth or Fiction?

Fact 3

Only the Catholic Douay Rheims and the kjv Bibles use the title "Holy Ghost." All other versions of the Bible call the third person of the Trinity by the title "Holy Spirit."

Will The Real Holy Ghost Please Stand Up

I have a faithful servant, who is also my student director. I gave her an assignment, which I have charged her to write and to give to you, the Redeemed; so that you, too, may write the vision and learn along with us.

The assignment is given to show you that **I Am Come to reverse the curses of the TEN PLAGUES** that Jehovah the God of mischief placed on Egypt. To start, I will break the curse of **"Water Into Blood"** that casts a spell of dumbness and disunity amongst the Black nation. Arise and be SMART! and go forth in your intelligence to REUNITE in solidarity with yOur first Godhead.

To guide your footstep back to the right path, I have given you a mysterious pictograph. Your homework is to solve it by researching the words "Holy" and "Ghost." **Write down your findings; and bring Me back an answer to My question: "Why is The Holy Ghost portrayed and accepted as a "white dove"?"**

Take another look at the pictograph and COME...Let us learn the lesson that will scatter Shem and Japheth....

Make Sure To Cross Reference With **TEN PLAGUES PLACED ON EGYPT: MURDERING OUR GODHEAD**

The Lord God Alpha Khen Omega, as dictated to Angela Powell

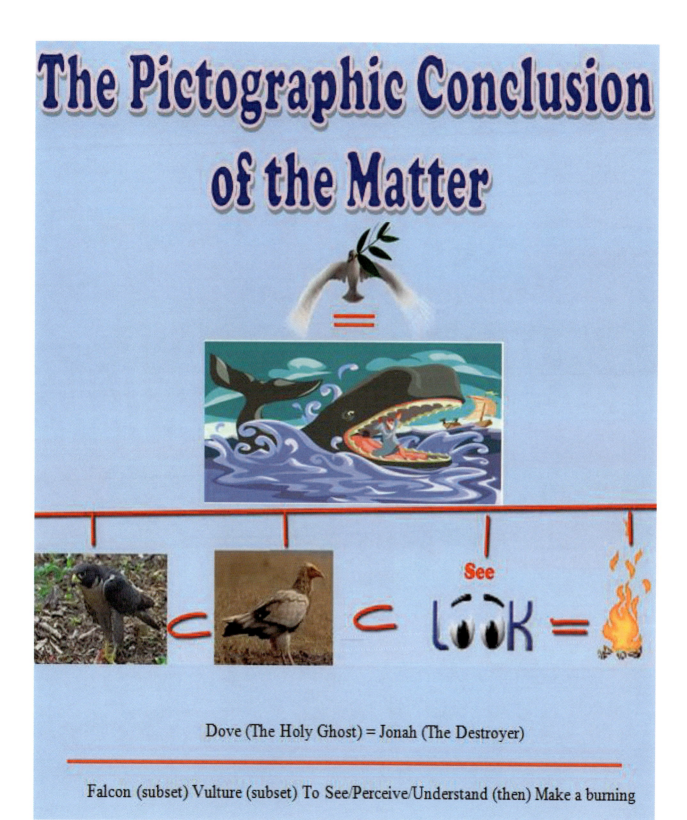

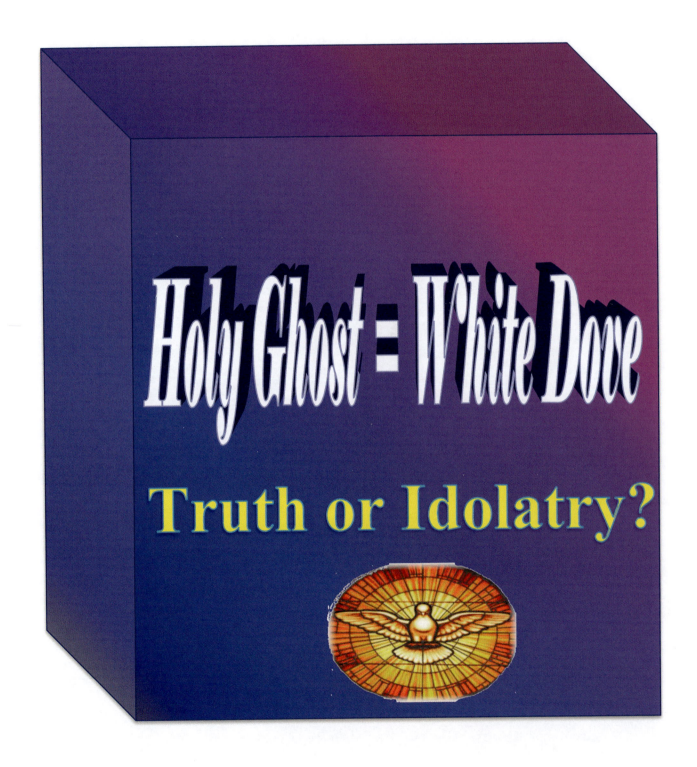

WORD STUDY
Dove = Jonah = Destroyer = Effervesce

DOVE = (Hebrew #3123) **yownah** - probably from the same as 3196; a dove (apparently from the warmth of their mating):--dove, pigeon. See Hebrew 3196

(H3196). **yayin** - from an unused root meaning to **effervesce**; wine (as fermented); by implication, intoxication:--banqueting, wine, wine(-bibber).

(H3120) **Yavan** - probably from the same as H3196; **effervescing** (i.e. hot and active); **Javan**, the name of a son of **Joktan**, and of the race (Ionians, i.e. Greeks) descended from him, with their territory; also of a place in Arabia:--Javan. See Hebrew 3196

3121. **yaven** - from the same as 3196; properly, dregs (as effervescing); hence, mud:--mire, miry. See Hebrew 3196

3124. **Yonah** - the same as H3123; **Jonah**, an Israelite:--Jonah. See Hebrew 3123

Yonah = Jonah or Jonas, **a dove;** he that oppresses; *DESTROYER* (Hitchcock Bible Name, HBN)

Question:

Is The Holy Ghost a "*Destroyer*" bird?

Make Sure To Cross Reference With TEN PLAGUES PLACED ON EGYPT: MURDERING OUR GODHEAD

The Lord God Alpha Khen Omega, as dictated to Angela Powell

Let us more thoroughly look into the matter.

Recall from **10 PLAGUES PLACED ON EGYPT** that "whale" is an "orca," which means "To Dig."

So, Wordsmith-- Prophet of the most high God, Get out your books and START…DIGGING…FOR…THOSE…WORDS…

Dig until you understand and can answer My question: "Why is The Holy Ghost portrayed and accepted as a "white dove"?"

WORD STUDY

Destroyer = To Burn Javan/Joktan/Japheth

"**Effervesce**" = bhreu-. Important derivatives are: brew, bread, broth, brood, breed, ferment, and fervent (AHD).

To boil, bubble, **effervesce**, **burn**; with derivatives referring to cooking and brewing.

Conclusion: Key Words

Holy Ghost/Dove: Jonah = Destroyer = effervesce = Javan/ Joktan/Japheth {Shem} = To Burn

Will The Real Holy Ghost Please Stand Up

The Scripture of Truth tells us that The Holy Ghost descended "like" a "dove" and lighted upon The Son of God, and REMAINED on Him.

The Scripture of Truth also states that "before Mary and Joseph came together, **Mary was found with child of The Holy Ghost."**

You, Redeemed, are a Christian-- a believer in The Father, The Son, and The Holy Ghost. The first question that *should* come to your mind after reading the above passages is: Who is The Holy Ghost? and, How accurate is the "white dove" image of Him? and, **How far back in time can I trace a sure-fire portrayal of a dove-like bird REMAINING (Resting) on The Son of God?"**

One method of arriving at an answer is to define "Son of God." "Son of God" comes from the Egyptian word "Sa Ra," which means "Son of Rā/God." "Sa Ra" also means "Pharaoh."

Now that you know The Scripture of Truth tells you about the life of a certain Pharaoh, to find a resolution for a historical depiction of what did the ancient people see when a dove-like bird lighted and remained on the Pharaoh, you must of necessity look into **10,000 years' worth of history** to locate the Pharaoh who has a "dove-like" Bird remaining upon him.

Make Sure To Cross Reference With **TEN PLAGUES PLACED ON EGYPT: MURDERING OUR GODHEAD**

The Lord God Alpha Khen Omega, as dictated to Angela Powell

2015 Will The Real Holy Ghost Please Stand Up

The heirs of Shem and Japheth call this Pharaoh with the dove-like bird REMAINING (Resting) upon him, Pharaoh Khafre. Even though he is worth studying, please do not digress from the purpose of your search. Therefore, RIGHT NOW keep your focus on The Holy Ghost.

As you can see, the bird that lighted on Pharaoh Khafre and remains on him is a falcon.

Is it possible that the words "Dove" and "Falcon" are interchangeable? *After all, as a bird of prey, a falcon is more of a "destroyer" than a dove.*

Should Scripture then read "Falcon" instead of "Dove?"

COME... Let us learn the lesson that will scatter Shem and Japheth....

Make Sure To Cross Reference With **TEN PLAGUES PLACED ON EGYPT: MURDERING OUR GODHEAD**

The Lord God Alpha Khen Omega, as dictated to Angela Powell

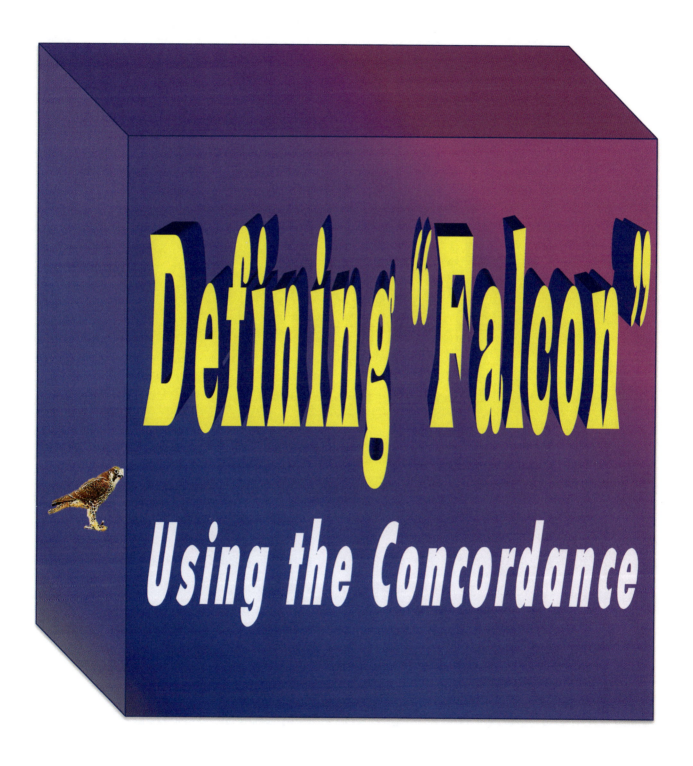

WORD STUDY

Dove/Falcon = Vulture = To See

H1772. dayah - intensive from **H1675**; a falcon (from its rapid flight):--vulture. See Hebrew 1675

1675. da'ah - a primitive root; to dart, i.e. fly rapidly:--fly.

1676. da'ah - from 1675; the kite (from its rapid flight):--vulture. See H7201. See Hebrew 1675; {See: Page 83}

H7201. ra'ah - from 7200; a bird of prey (probably the vulture, from its sharp sight):--glede. Compare 1676. See Hebrew 7200; See Hebrew 1676

H7200. ra'ah - a primitive root; to see, literally or figuratively (in numerous applications, direct and implied, transitive, intransitive and causative):--advise self, appear, approve, behold, X certainly, consider, discern, (make to) enjoy, have experience, gaze, take heed, X indeed, X joyfully, lo, look (on, one another, one on another, one upon another, out, up, upon), mark, meet, X be near, perceive, present, provide, regard, (have) respect, (fore-, cause to, let) see(-r, -m, one another), shew (self), X sight of others, (e-)spy, stare, X surely, X think, view, visions.

Key Words: da'ah = falcon = vulture = ra'ah, To See

The Lord God Alpha Khen Omega, as dictated to Angela Powell

A Parable: Eye of Rā + Vulture

Parable Message:

Holy Ghost/Dove/Falcon (Vulture{kjv}): =

To See = (Eye of Re) + vulture.

In order to understand the portrait of a "Dove-like" bird that rests upon The Son of God, you need **"To SEE"** an ancient "Falcon/Vulture"

Solution: Eye of Rā + Vulture

Dove = Falcon = Vulture = (Ra'ah) To See

Matthew 10:16

¶ Behold, I send you forth as sheep in the midst of wolves: **be ye therefore wise as serpents, and harmless as doves.**

The Lord God Alpha Khen Omega, as dictated to Angela Powell

The Aten Speaks: Team Atenites.

Redeemed, **GO!**
"Do you SEE one of MY Mysteries?"

Dove=Falcon=Vulture=(Ra'ah) To See

I wrote it thousands of years ago, and kept it a secret~~just for this dispensation… to be opened by you…

A spell of dumbness-until-death has been casted upon you. ~~**ARISE**~~ and shake it off!

Can't SEE the mystery? Or, Don't understand it just, yet? No problem! Gather in teams~~**Team Atenites**~~ and use this book as a study guide on how to divinely command ancient texts to manifest their secrets so that you may SEE **The WORD of God** in action as it commands The Real Holy Ghost To Please Stand UP for you, the Redeemed!

In the Hieroglyphics, the Vulture is Mut, Who is Isis. But again, even though Isis is worth studying, do not digress from the assignment at hand. Keep your focus solely on The Holy Ghost.

It is time to open some Scriptures…

Your first introduction to The Holy Ghost comes from Matthew 1:18.

Let us go there…

For Visual Tutorials Visit: AlphaKhenOmegaNews on YouTube.com

Instructions for Interpreting "The Virgin Birth" Parable

> Matthew 1:18
>
> ¶ Now the birth of Jesus Christ was on this wise: When as his mother Mary was espoused to Joseph, before they came together, ==she was found with child of the Holy Ghost.==

I, The Son of God, speak in parables, as is written in Matthew 13:34-35. The whole story of the birth of Jesus Christ, The Son of God, born to the virgin Mary, begotten of The Holy Ghost, is a parable that occurred in ancient Egypt and is set in stone on the pyramid walls.

Come…I will send the multitude away, so that I may declare unto you, the parable of the "Virgin Birth," starting with Matthew 1:1 and concluding with the last verse of that Chapter, which is 1:25.

I will follow the technique you learned in **THE 10 PLAGUES PLACED ON EGYPT.** Only this time, we will brandish our **sharp Two-edged sword,** which means we will declare Right-Now-Words that have power to cut off our enemies, scatter them, and reverse the hands of our captivity.

With our Two-edged sword, **firstly,** we will list the corresponding Scriptures. **Secondly,** we will reinterpret the given Hebrew verses into RIGHT NOW English. **Thirdly,** we shall see what I, The Lord God Alpha Khen Omega, have to say on the matter.

 Make Sure To Cross Reference With **TEN PLAGUES PLACED ON EGYPT: MURDERING OUR GODHEAD**

The Lord God Alpha Khen Omega, as dictated to Angela Powell

Biblical References: Revelation 1:16 – RIGHT NOW Words

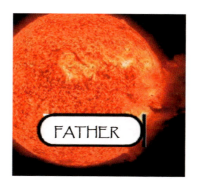

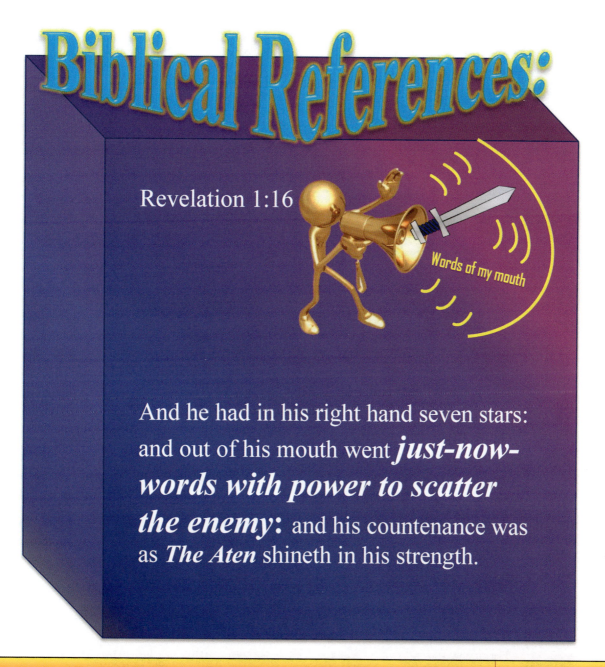

Revelation 1:16

Words of my mouth

And he had in his right hand seven stars: and out of his mouth went *just-now-words with power to scatter the enemy:* and his countenance was as *The Aten* shineth in his strength.

The Lord God Alpha Khen Omega, as dictated to Angela Powell

MESSAGE IN HEBRAIC TONGUE

Shem and Japheth as representing the Caucasoid races

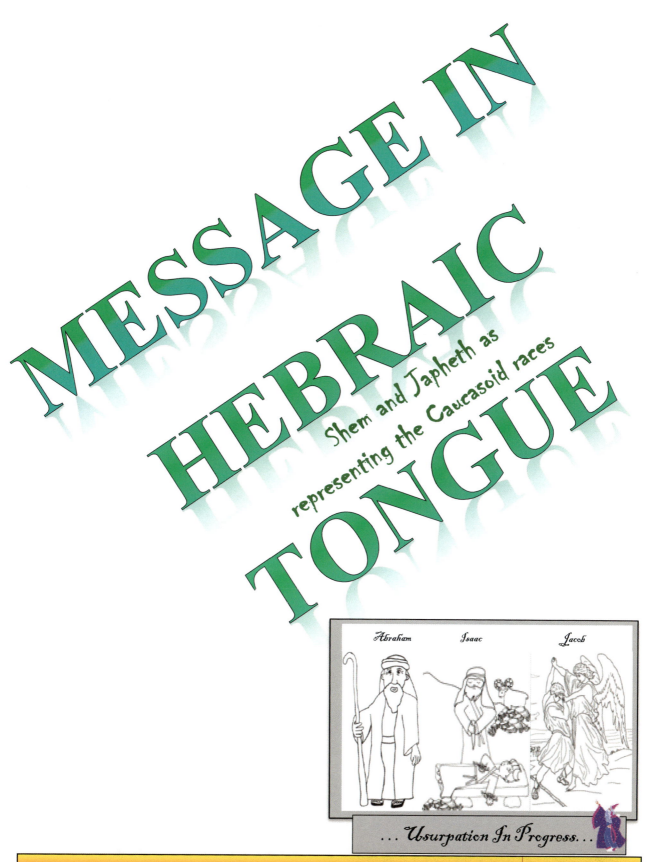

Abraham Isaac Jacob

...Usurpation In Progress...

Sociolinguists' Biblical Interpretations:

Matthew 1:1 – 25 {Possibly plagiarized from ancient Hieroglyphics)

1   The book of the generation of Jesus Christ, the son of David, the son of Abraham.

2   Abraham begat Isaac; and Isaac begat Jacob; and Jacob begat Judas and his brethren;

3   And Judas begat Phares and Zara of Thamar; and Phares begat Esrom; and Esrom begat Aram;

4   And Aram begat Aminadab; and Aminadab begat Naasson; and Naasson begat Salmon;

5   And Salmon begat Booz of Rachab; and Booz begat Obed of Ruth; and Obed begat Jesse;

6   And Jesse begat David the king; and David the king begat Solomon of her that had been the wife of Urias;

7   And Solomon begat Roboam; and Roboam begat Abia; and Abia begat Asa;

8   And Asa begat Josaphat; and Josaphat begat Joram; and Joram begat Ozias;

9   And Ozias begat Joatham; and Joatham begat Achaz; and Achaz begat Ezekias;

Make Sure To Cross Reference With **TEN PLAGUES PLACED ON EGYPT: MURDERING OUR GODHEAD**

Sociolinguists' Biblical Interpretations:

Matthew 1:1 – 25 (Cont'd)

10 And Ezekias begat Manasses; and Manasses begat Amon; and Amon begat Josias;

11 And Josias begat Jechonias and his brethren, about the time they were carried away to Babylon:

12 And after they were brought to Babylon, Jechonias begat Salathiel; and Salathiel begat Zorobabel;

13 And Zorobabel begat Abiud; and Abiud begat Eliakim; and Eliakim begat Azor;

14 And Azor begat Sadoc; and Sadoc begat Achim; and Achim begat Eliud;

15 And Eliud begat Eleazar; and Eleazar begat Matthan; and Matthan begat Jacob;

16 And Jacob begat Joseph the husband of Mary, of whom was born Jesus, who is called Christ.

17 So all the generations from Abraham to David are fourteen generations; and from David until the carrying away into Babylon are fourteen generations; and from the carrying away into Babylon unto Christ are fourteen generations.

Sociolinguists' Biblical Interpretations:

Matthew 1:1 – 25 (Cont'd)

18 Now the birth of Jesus Christ was on this wise: When as his mother Mary was espoused to Joseph, before they came together, <mark>she was found with child of the Holy Ghost.</mark>

19 Then Joseph her husband, being a just man, and not willing to make her a publick example, was minded to put her away privily.

20 But while he thought on these things, behold, the angel of the Lord appeared unto him in a dream, saying, Joseph, thou son of David, fear not to take unto thee Mary thy wife: for that which is conceived in her is of the Holy Ghost.

21 And she shall bring forth a son, and thou shalt call his name JESUS: for he shall save his people from their sins.

22 Now all this was done, that it might be fulfilled which was spoken of the Lord by the prophet, saying,

23 Behold, a virgin shall be with child, and shall bring forth a son, and they shall call his name Emmanuel, which being interpreted is, God with us.

24 Then Joseph being raised from sleep did as the angel of the Lord had bidden him, and took unto him his wife:

25 And knew her not till she had brought forth her firstborn son: and he called his name JESUS.

Make Sure To Cross Reference With **TEN PLAGUES PLACED ON EGYPT: MURDERING OUR GODHEAD**

The Lord God Alpha Khen Omega, as dictated to Angela Powell

The Nativity: OPENING A MYSTERY

Matthew 1:18

¶ Now the birth **(Nativity = Lod)** of Jesus Christ was on this wise: When as his

mother Mary, **Rebellion (HBN)**

was espoused to Joseph, Revealer of secrets, I know who you are! You were brought into My country by My fat bull of Africa, chief of the executioners. Your god is a dog-headed, frog-faced, ape-god name Amen the Devil. I have given you peril and misfortune for a wife and your first fruit shall be those who are forgotten. Your father-in-law is he who demolishes the fat of Jacob to the end that he may scatter the enemy abroad, and cast your God of mischief into the Lake of Fire burning with brimstone **(Heb/Grk Concord)**.

before they came together,

she was found with child of

the Holy Ghost **Ail: that is to say the Holy Ghost of the (Eagle {Dan/Lud/Nativity}) Terah**.

~~~ STOP ~~~

The Power Of Writing Down My Thoughts: Test Yourself Journaling Page

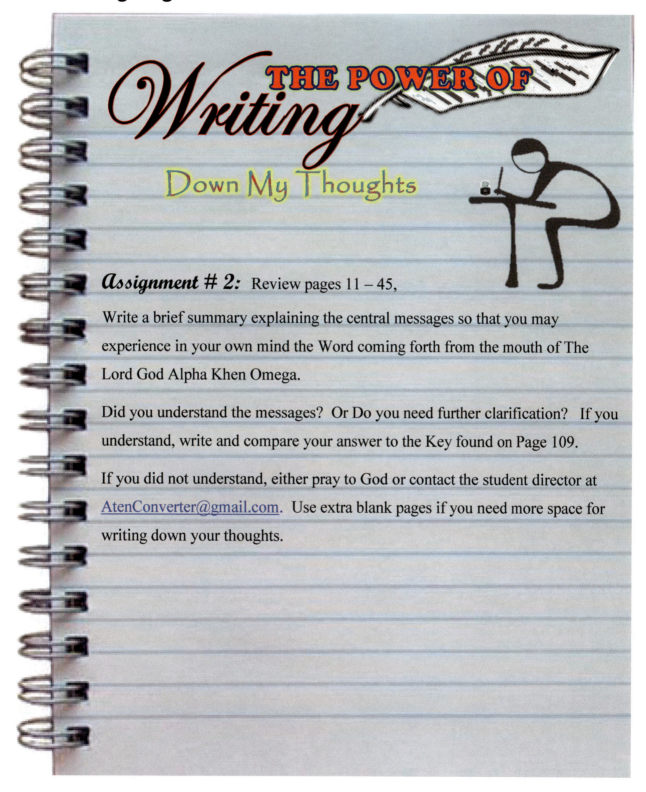

Assignment # 2: Review pages 11 – 45,

Write a brief summary explaining the central messages so that you may experience in your own mind the Word coming forth from the mouth of The Lord God Alpha Khen Omega.

Did you understand the messages? Or Do you need further clarification? If you understand, write and compare your answer to the Key found on Page 109.

If you did not understand, either pray to God or contact the student director at AtenConverter@gmail.com. Use extra blank pages if you need more space for writing down your thoughts.

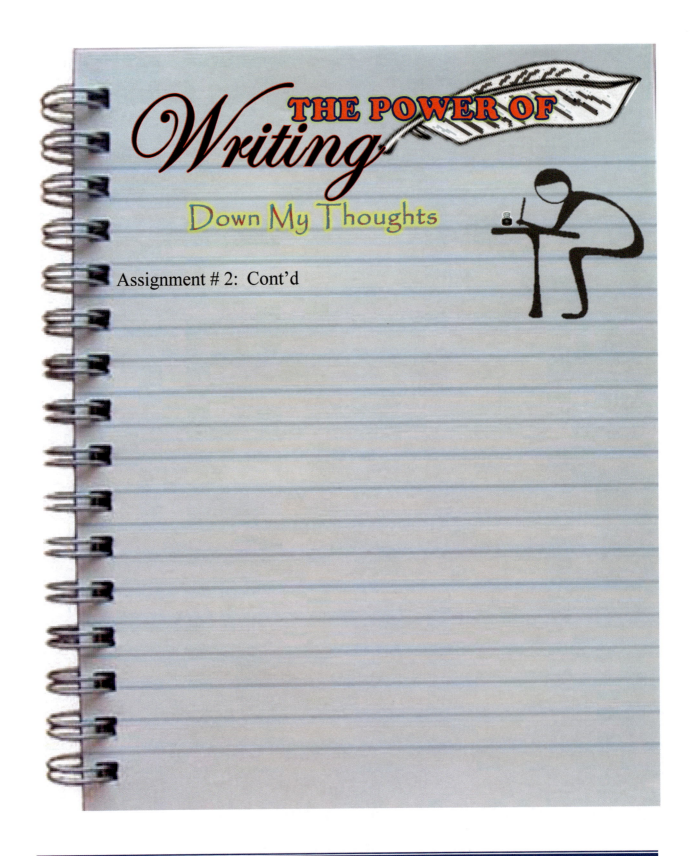

The Lord God Alpha Khen Omega, as dictated to Angela Powell

MESSAGE IN HAMITIC TONGUE

Ham as representative of the African/Egyptian

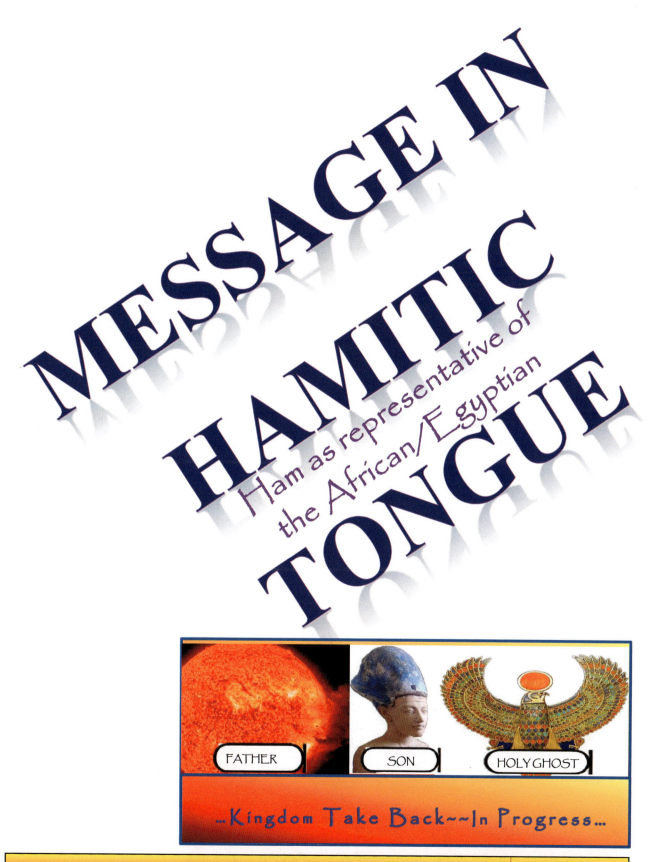

FATHER · SON · HOLY GHOST

...Kingdom Take Back~~In Progress...

The Aten Speaks: Introducing The True Deliverer

Matthew 1:1 – 25 with emphasis on verse 18

Team Atenites,

This is the papyrus/book of the nativity of a Deliverer: He is the well-beloved, Pharaoh Akhenaton. Not born in bondage, he is freedom's most powerful fermentation. He is violently hurling in a time of turbulence and confusion upon Javan, son of Japheth, elder brother of Shem, who are sons of Noah, who is son of Jehovah the God of mischief.

AS for the Deliverer: The buckle on the cheek strap of His helmet is **RIGHT NOW** piercing through the armor of the Shemetic and Japhetic warriors. Every battle of the warrior is with confused noise and garments rolled in blood; but his piercing is fueled by the burning fires of a massive coronal ejection from the Sun of Heaven; that is to say, from Me, The Aten. Redemption for the enslaved is the catalyst for His coming back into being, which is called **The Second Coming**.

His papyrus is to be opened and published by a virtuous Black woman, who shall be His binding director. Being guided by dreams and visions, the director copies the words with their definitions from the Book of Matthew, which allows her to write about the nativity of My Son~~ The Son of God/Aten. For the purpose of this literature, The Son is Pharaoh Amen'hotep IV, being called Pharaoh Akhenaton, being called Jesus Christ, the first begotten of the dead Who was conceived by The Holy Ghost and born of a virgin, which thing is a Mystery.

He is The Lord God Alpha Khen Omega.

The Deliverer commanded, then equipped, the director to define the term "The Holy Ghost." Supplied with sufficient equipment, The Deliverer sent the director on a quest to thoroughly read many out-of-print books until she can arrive at a concrete definition for— or a true visual portrayal of... what you, the Redeemed, should expect to see in your visual perception of The Holy Ghost. This: OR This:

The Author (Pharaoh Akhenaton), Whom we call our Deliver/Savior, dictates His autobiography to the director via DNA/RNA transcription. In the night, while the director sleeps, the transcription takes place. In the morning, when she rises, she learns to translate the transcription. And though this particular director is yet learning how to respond~~for the sake of Godspeed...**RIGHT NOW**...for the purposes of overcoming evil, The Word of God authorizes the writing, editing, and publishing of His new words based solely upon the old. The director is being trained to bring you, the Redeemed, a well-defined script using the theories put forth in "generative grammar" to publish His real life-story as it unfolds during The Second Coming happening in this moment in time.

FATHER

My Words are the accumulated works of many virtuous Black women, who seek My face and serve Me as My binding director.

The Power of Writing Down My Thoughts: Test Yourself Journaling Page

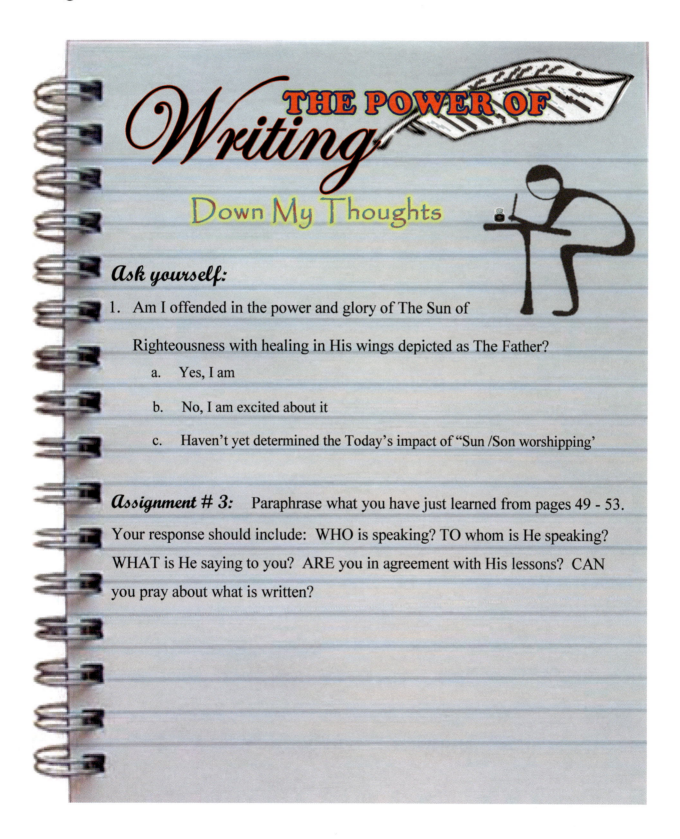

THE POWER OF Writing Down My Thoughts

Ask yourself:

1. Am I offended in the power and glory of The Sun of Righteousness with healing in His wings depicted as The Father?
   a. Yes, I am
   b. No, I am excited about it
   c. Haven't yet determined the Today's impact of "Sun /Son worshipping'

Assignment # 3: Paraphrase what you have just learned from pages 49 - 53. Your response should include: WHO is speaking? TO whom is He speaking? WHAT is He saying to you? ARE you in agreement with His lessons? CAN you pray about what is written?

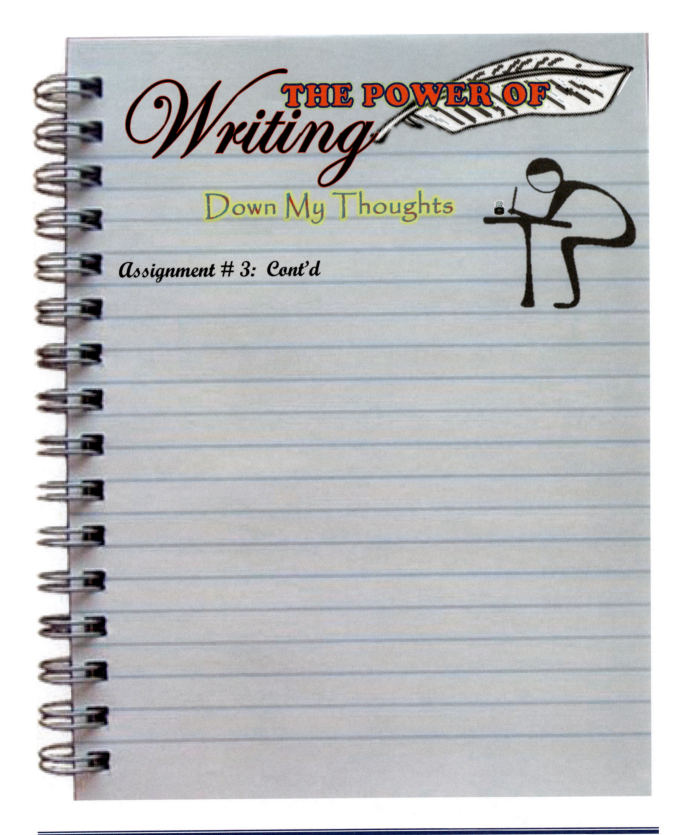

**The Aten Speaks On:
The Kerygma of "Lod"**

```
          ┌─── Ludim (Gen. 10:13)
   Lod ───┤
          └─── Lud (Gen. 10:22)
```

As for the "Birth Chart" on the obverse side of this page: It is saying: the Hebrew word used for "birth" is "nativity." **The Bible name that means "nativity" is "Lod."** In addition to being Kabbalistic onomancy (Jewish name divination), in the field of Sociolinguistics, **Lod shows an example of how language and society intersect to shape the social, speaking, psychological, and in this case, religious, nature of parties involved in biblical development. Said groups or parties use language to set themselves apart from others tribes.** They hold within themselves a superiority resulting from their society's control over the minds and tongues of those tribes who must conform to their abnormalities and twisted lies when seeking G (-g)od-inspired words.

Verily, verily, the name "Ludim" is used first in Scripture before it is usurped by "Lud." That means: **The birth of Jesus Christ should truly begin with the genealogy of Ludim, which comes from the lineage of Ham.** Regardless of that truth, Shemetic and Japhetic sociolinguists that practice name divination, wrestle with God to twist the nativity story away from Ludim. Ludim is Mizraim's first son. Mizraim is Ham's second son and it is also the biblical name of ancient of Egypt. Sociolinguists refer to all of Africa as the land of Ham by way of Mizraim.

Ludim is Ham's firstborn grandson by Mizraim. Once the sociolinguists twisted the nativity story, they changed it over to a binding outcome favorable to Shem's fourth-born son, Lud.

Make Sure To Cross Reference With **TEN PLAGUES PLACED ON EGYPT: MURDERING OUR GODHEAD**

The Lord God Alpha Khen Omega, as dictated to Angela Powell

In Lud, you find kidnappers snatching Abraham's kinsmen. Abraham pursues the kidnappers into Dan and takes back (**redeem**) his klan without paying silver or gold. If there is a lesson to learn from Abraham the thief, it is that he trains 318 servants in his own house to be armed warriors in his own private army. The warriors are able to rescue anything taken from Abraham. They are also ruthless enough to corral evil spirits to help them conquer, suppress, enslave and control innocent men. Using the powers of dark forces, they become high father and rulers over the multitude of the Hamitic seed whom they oppress, to this day.

Not leaving his household or belongings behind, as commanded by Jehovah-- his God of mischief, Abraham and his warriors pursued kidnappers all the way through Israel until they reached Dan. That is to say: For four generations (280 years), Abraham and his warriors wrestled with Aten, God the Creator, so that they can rule as God/Israel. The name **"Israel" means "he will rule as God."** Israel's sinful striving is righteousness (Dan) in his own eyes, and impiously, the sociolinguists of the biblical patriarchs snatch the nativity away from Ham and hand it over to Shem who co-rules with his brother, Japheth the elder.

Jacob is Israel. The name **"Jacob" means both "supplanter; and James."** The name **"Israel" also means "he who wrestles with God."** The name **"Dan" means "righteousness."** The name **"Abraham" means "naked, strong thief."** Hence, through his descendants up to Dan, you find the naked thief wrestling with God the Creator until his inferiority becomes righteous superiority in his own eyes, as well as the eyes of his sociolinguists who retell his stories.

Keep in mind, Shem's and Japheth's powers are limited to social, linguistic, and religious foreigners who accept and live under their viewpoints about their biblical patriarchs. You, the melanoid Redeemed, are called to a higher sphere of spirituality wherein you SEE beyond the twisted lies to KNOW the truth. Truth is Māa-t.

Like as Lud is fourth-born son of Shem; Canaan is fourth-born son of Ham. Noah curses Canaan to be a servant of servants to Shem and Japheth. **Via Lud (the Shemetic nativity) Shem and Japheth get to direct the biblical manuscript that both binds Canaan in perpetual slavery and replaces the Hamitic nativity with Shemetic nativity.** In that way, when Shem and Japheth come to take Canaan into captivity for a third time, the prejudicial indoctrinations of their sociolinguists affirm to the denizens in their enlarged communities that kidnapping and holding Black men in captivity is their god-given birthright.

But let us see what saith I, Pharaoh Akhenaton-in-My-new name-The Lord God Alpha Khen Omega…

~~~~PROCEEDing WITH THE INTERPRETATION~~~~

The Aten Speaks:
Answering Rachel

I have indeed judged you, thus said The Lord God Alpha Khen Omega. Your psychedelic vision is as clear as the god of the sky during the twilight of a Tuesday evening in July; but, you could not see that your father, Abraham-- the naked, strong thief, pursued captivity captive until he reached Dan. I drove him there and allowed him to go no further. Your son, Dan, was begotten of your maid, who was old and confused. What came from her was predestined to be confounded with roots that utterly wither away as herbage underneath Me, the parching sun. The righteousness you seek is a dried up waterbed.

Rachel, you are venomous; you spread poison among My people to cause them to worship your gods of mischief, which thing ensnares them in your net of bondage. You find enjoyment in their captivity and are eager with excitement to steal all their gold; even the gold that is God's work.

The time of Dan is now, your Judgement is here! The third period of captivity you prophesied against My saints failed because your righteousness comes from confused noise of brandishing a sacrificial wave offering of abominable animals to gods of mischief who answer your prayers with tumultuous signs from the sky. I abhor you and your offerings.

Though you shine for Zeus and are a descendant of Jupiter, I Am come to bind the diadem of your power. The third angel is sounding…Can't you hear him, O female ewe on a journey to the seat of the gods on Mount Olympus! Write in your diary that the root of your gall and wormwood is now cut off from My people. Ye and your star, Diana, shall drink of the fountains of waters made bitter by your own Wormwood. Because of the bitterness you have spewed against My great name, many of your men shall choose to drink your bitter waters and die rather than to taste My sweet living water and live.

Make Sure To Cross Reference With TEN PLAGUES PLACED ON EGYPT: MURDERING OUR GODHEAD

I Am even RIGHT NOW taking away your Savior, Jesus Christ, and destroying your idol, your White Dove of Peace, when there was never any peace for the saints of God. I Am even RIGHT NOW bringing to naught the works of those who give the backs of their bodies for the sorcerers and talismans to mount upon in order to rise up against Me.

In secret you scratched out your own interpretation of the Scriptures, yeah, you changed My Word. Let, now, the silence of your muted justice system grate on your mind: Apollyon, the Destroyer, plucked away the place where Heru is extolled, like one plucks a bird. His great eclipse destroyed Heru's City like as the calamity following a furious thunderstorm. Ye, knowing it, kept it secret and allowed what was holy to be replanted with something horrible and destined to destruction and perdition.

Ye have given your backs to Apollyon~~ call him Apollonopolis Magna or Apollo Superior~~ he remains no more than Saatt ta, Set, Aapep, Apophis, Satan, Jehovah the God of mischief, Zeus, your Father~~ Amen the Devil.

For all this, I Am NOT appeased: for you stole the nativity from Mizraim-- My land of great respect for authority. You besieged His throne: for which cause your affliction shall be with swords and flames…fire that cometh down from God out of Heaven to devour you of Gog and Magog when you go out with your father to war against Me.

Had you paid Mizraim a mouthful of bread, My day's work against you should be fulfilled; but He has a mouthful of dough: for My hand has just begun to pierce the sphere of your White Knight. When My saints see him trodden down, their hopes of life shall begin anew. My Word to them from the hand of My scribe is sweet; but to you it is Wormwood: for I desire that you could-- but you cannot-- change your evil ways. Therefore, the Destroyer has chosen you and ye have chosen him, Apollyon.

Thinketh ye, that 911, is a mere lone attack on America? 9-1-1 is the beginning of your woes! It is your calling forth of Apollyon! It is your readying for the War of Gog and Magog! Hear ye not how that after a long binding, Satan-in-his-name-Jehovah is released from prison just to gather his children together in a war of the races against Me, The Aten? I Am the Maker and Creator of the Heavens, the Earth, the Seas, and all that therein is! I create the good and the evil! Think you that your sun god, Apollo, can destroy Me, The Sun of Righteousness…The Aten?

Apollo is your Great Colonizer; ye call on him to enslave the Redeemed. Ye plot with him to cultivate a master city beyond the firmaments, using My people to till the barren grounds of Mars. Shall ye win? Nay, but ye shall heap to yourselves woes upon woes, The horns have changed-- whereas you thought to enslave My people yet again, the iron yokes of captivity be upon your necks… *like Haman hanging from the gallows…* your "reversal Alpha share!"

Hanging, ye shall seek death, but death shall flee from thee! There is nothing left for thee but weeping and gnashing of teeth.

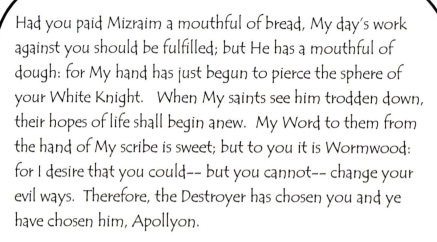

Make Sure To Cross Reference With **TEN PLAGUES PLACED ON EGYPT, MURDERING OUR GODHEAD**

The Lord God Alpha Khen Omega, as dictated to Angela Powell

~~~~START AT THE TRUE NATIVITY~~~~

Changing Lanes from Shem and Japheth over to Ham

Opening A Mystery, Page 45 Cont'd

(Matt. 1:18) ¶ Now the birth (**Nativity = Lod/Ludim**) of Jesus/ A Savior-- not born in bondage... and a Deliverer Who helps **Canaan** when you cry out for freedom from your bondage—came; and is here again, **RIGHT NOW!** ...The Second Coming... Christ anointed Black Messiah was on this wise:

....SECOND COMING....

See: SECOUDINES

> Canaan
> is
> New Jerusalem
> is
> The Lamb's Bride

~~~~ STOP ~~~~

The Power of Writing Down My Thoughts

Assignment # 4: Paraphrase pages 57 – 65; incorporate it with Assignments # 1, 2, and 3, so that you may experience in your own mind the Word coming forth from the mouth of The Lord God Alpha Khen Omega. Compare your answer to the Answer Key on page 110. Use extra blank pages, if needed, to write down your answer.

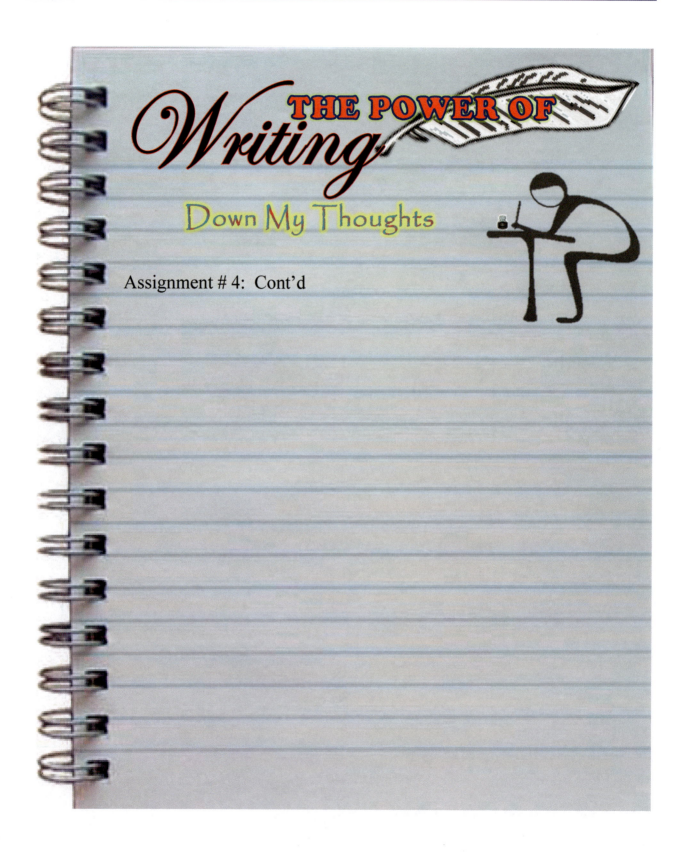

Arise From Your Comfort Zone

Team Atenites

ready.set.go

Daily News

22 December 2015... 04:49
Orange Coast College, Costa Mesa, California

Philosophy 100

On March 1994, Professor Badcock gave his epic lecture and engaged his students in the age-old debate as to whether or not Blacks are the "CURSE OF HAM?"

Professor Badcock challenged the one, lone, Black student in attendance of his international student body to write a thesis on the topic, which would become her passing "or failing" grade.

During an interview with the student, 21 years after that bullying event, Daily News discovered that the student thoroughly researched the subject and with careful prayer over her findings, she discovered that the professor was one in a line of many who is RIGHT NOW planning to enslave the Redeemed on Mars. As a result, the student has gone on to become an advocate for spiritual conversion away from Jehovah the God of mischief over to The Aten, The God of Righteousness with healing in His Wings; Who delivers the enslaved out of curses and bondage.

Fact 5

Regarding the "Captivity in Egypt," the Book of Genesis reveals that Jacob started out with 72 souls in the Land of Ham. From that number came 600,000 "footmen" (taskmasters). The rest of the people in captivity were Black people who sold themselves into the hand of Jehovah the God of mischief so that he would let them live during a severer famine that he brought upon the land to kill or enslave the native peoples. That is why you need "REDEMPTION reactivated!"

~~~~BEGIN INTERPRETATION~~~~Two-Edged Sword
Scriptural Translation Comes Directly to you from The Lord God Alpha Khen Omega

During the fall of man, there arose **a naked, strong thief** who began to mock The Aten and to wrestle with The Aten so that he could usurp The Aten and rule as God in place of The Aten. **He broke through the cover of a sarcophagus and beheld the holy story, which became his Jewish confession.** Because the naked, strong thief and his God of mischief made a breach in the holy of holies and began to plagiarize the holy story, I plagued them with the plague of leprosy in their flesh that made them appear in color like unto the palm of the hand. But they were not deterred. They begat trumpeters to surround My Kingdom with a stockade and they attacked My crown. They were not a part of Me, therefore, caused I a separation between their country and Mine.

Those alien lepers began to deceive My people and to place curses upon them. They compelled volunteer soldiers to go throughout the world with enchantments, and to whisper magic spells that would begin their curses of captivity. Via the spells, the military~~dressed in the travesty of blackface and transvestitism~~ besieged My throne.

The blackface transvestites built a strong pillar in front of the temple in quarrelsome Egypt, where they **chose most sweetest Canaan to inflict with curses that bound Canaan in bondage to travesties of blackface transvestites.**

In strength, they made Canaanites to till the ground and their shepherdesses became drunken and satisfied with captivity, so much so that they began to evil entreat Canaan.

In hard bondage and confusion of face, Canaanites began to call on Jehovah

the God of mischief. As a result, you all have come to believe that you exist because of the goodness of Jehovah the God of mischief~~ your Adversary. .

To conquer the world and infuse it with his religion, Jehovah the God of mischief established a well-beloved king who became the foundation of power in Islam. The base of his power was a Muslim daughter who has a seven times oath sworn of the people of the God of terror. The daughter of oath is the wife of flame-- a fire and a light of Jah of the East.

They are a people who commit adultery with Egypt to fulfil the curse placed on Canaan. Speaking magic words, the enchanters force, open-wide the bowels of Canaan until the adulterers transformed unsuspecting Canaan into a worshipping people overshadowed by the God of mischief and violence; who comes to devour the holy seed and harshly judge them with a binding curse that entraps and sentences them to bondage.

Though the adulterers were stripped of their strength and cursed with leprosy in their flesh as the color like unto the color of the palm of the hand that did not deter sweetest and innocent Canaan from trusting in adulterers who come to devour their holiness.

Together with daughters of Jehovah the God of mischief, Canaan began to breed worms-- heirs trusting in lepers. The children of leprosy made Jehovah the God of mischief complete.

Then came Jehovah the God of mischief to occupy Canaan...physically and spiritually...by driving out Canaan's previous holy and divine tenants. Islam of Jah-of-the-East, the Sadducees and priests of Jehovah the God of mischief, along with their military dressed in the travesty of blackface and transvestitism, took possession of Canaan's souls, which made it easy for them to besiege the throne of Mizraim-- the home of the falcon's nest, the dwelling place of Egypt's Holy Ghost.

The adulterers, using the strength of Gods of mischief, seized Canaan and then Egypt and then Ham and then his countries round about him. The leprous occupants-- the adulterers, stayed until they cause Canaan to forget....in

forgetfulness...forget what...?

> **REMEMBER AND FORGET NOT**
>
> The graven images of their gods shall ye burn with fire (Deut. 7:25);
>
> And thou shalt remember that thou wast a bondman in *the land of Anguish*: and thou shalt observe and do these statutes (Deut. 16:12):
>
> thou shalt cast away as a menstruous cloth *the covenant embedded within your Adversary's money*; thou shalt say unto it, Get thee hence (Isaiah 30:22).
>
> Atenites, Ask Me, your God "To weigh those who enslave you."

Cunning workmen and expert architects in the art of "causing to forget" establish the foundation of Jah:~~ It is the mechanical fires of Jehovah the God of mischief~~ Being a mode of knowledge, it replaces the Light of The Aten.

When the ears of the daughters of The Aten are adorned to witness for The Aten on a swell of ground where they can learn to hear God intelligently about what He, The Aten, has prepared for them to see and hear that comes from the cover of the sarcophagus that was stolen from them round about the time their forefathers renounced allegiance to their father's native land of Ham/Canaan/Egypt, the evil light of the God of mischief shall go out!

Upon their renouncement, they entered into the Confusion of Face in Abraham-- the naked strong thief. It is the wrongful place of the dark forces and occult, being called Ur of the Chaldees. After Canaan was brought to this place of confusion, which is chattel slavery, Jehovah the God of mischief sits him on his knee and rears him to say, "I am lent of God to be a bondman to Shem and Japheth until Jah the great redeems me." But

The Lord God Alpha Khen Omega, as dictated to Angela Powell

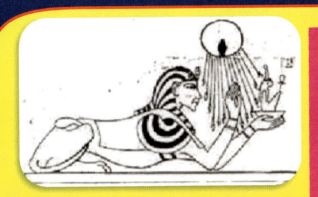

Jehovah shall never redeem Canaan.

Canaan's son was born in this confusion; he flows away and waxes warm in chattel slavery; in confusion he praises Jehovah the God of mischief; in confusion he calls the God of mischief his Father; and in confusion he awaits the resurrection of those who come from Abraham's wrongful place of dark forces and occults. It is the abode of evil and telepathic sorcerers. The evil daughters of the sorcerers speak in the gift of tongues and call forth the enslaved Canaanites with promises of redemption from the Lord of spiritual heights, who uses a Black succor that turns the Sadducee's unrighteousness into righteousness.

In the resurrection of Jehovah the god of mischief, the Black succor and Sadducees plagiarized ancient things that made the sun stand still. The power of the God of majesty~~The Aten, and his assistant, Lazarus, made the sun stand still when Lazarus was given… and received… the gift of life.

The plagiarizers stole the gift and gave it to the usurper, Jacob—who incarnates by name into James the king, who still wrestles with The Aten to rule as the Light of God. They gave also a present of war from Baal.

To James was added a son who possesses the spirit to breathe rebellion during the publishing of his binding directive that plagiarizes the cover of the sarcophagus. The director-- James of the god of mischief, wrote about the whole timeframe from the naked strong thief to the white knight; that is to say, the king of those who usurp.

The given period is 70 times 14 generations, which is to say 980 years. And from the time of the white knight until the renouncing of allegiance to Canaan's father's native land (which renouncement caused them to enter into the confusion of face in Abraham, the naked strong thief of the place of the dark forces and occult, being called Ur of the Chaldees, being called Babylon) is another 70 times 14 generations; which is to say, another 980 years. The timeframe then given comprises 1,960 years. And from the renouncing of allegiance to their father's native land to enter into

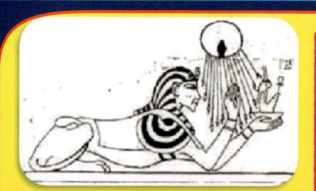

the confusion of face in Abraham, are 70 times 14 generations; which is to say, another 980 years; adding a total encompassing 2,940 years. {And from their white knight and his binding director-- being called Jesus and James-- until you who are captured in this chattel slavery are another 2015 years; which means from Abraham, the naked strong thief, unto you, the Bible covers a period of 4,955 years; plus, the thousands of years from the time of Adam unto Abraham, which the Book of Matthew did not list in the nativity of their white knight.

(Now on to Matthew 1:18)

The name "Matthew" means "to war." He fought with The Aten and prevailed to write about a woman named "Rebellion." "Mary" means "Miriam" and "Rebellion." The rebel woman's story comes from the cover of a sarcophagus depicting the rebellion of those who convene with the ram on their climbing up to the sun to bequest him to give to them a souvenir, which was the adding of another son. In addition to another son, it was agreed that before Rebellion and her husband could convene {marry and conceive}, they must agree to enter into a covenant stating: "Rebellion was found with child of the Ail: that is to say the Holy Ghost of the (Eagle) Terah: that is to say the father of Abraham. Madness shall come from plagiarizing the Hieroglyphics."

Rebellion brought forth a son-- a mocker, to mock The Son of The Aten. Her husband-- the diviner of secrets, called their son by that name which means: "Thou shalt hail and incite by authoritative word the character called Deliverer: For he shall SOS the whole tribe of the tomb of his people with a reversal Alpha share; that is to say, from the first man of Abraham up to Rebellion's added son, unto the war of unbinding their lies, what Rebellion wrought shall stand."

Now all this was to cause to be "gen"-erate, a society abundantly supplied with superior police that run and flow as water underneath white supremacy~~ masters under the authority of the fore-fire/light of all that Jehovah the god of mischief came to "lay" forth.

The Lord God Alpha Khen Omega, as dictated to Angela Powell

He whose name means "To War" wrote: Behold, The children of renowned name (Shem and Japheth) have a secret virgin.

He is a young man, the son of Mary; that is to say, son of Rebellion, and son of Jehovah god of mischief. He walks happily because he is a healer for his nation; but from the beginning, he is one who curses you in a captivity that lasts until I, The Lord God Alpha Khen Omega, come with the Two-edged sword, speaking RIGHT NOW Words from My mouth that scatter what Rebellion wrought back into the Lake of Fire with the gods of their dark forces and sorcery.

Upon the scattering, the secret of the children of a Black Virgin with a renowned name of Ham is that they are happy because a Healer-- a Pharaoh, Son of God, has come to release them from the generational curses put on them by Shem and Japheth.

With My sharp Two-edged sword, I shall cause the Black Virgin to birth from his mind, like the bringing forth of a son, a story about Emmanuel; which being interpreted is, God with us.

Then the Revealer of secrets, being raised from his spiritual torpor and awakened to visions that did guide him to do as the angel of The Aten had bidden him to do, and the Revealer of secrets did put away from him his wife named Rebellion and took unto him his wife, the Black Virgin: And can speak to her not again till she brings forth her first work: which is called PUBLISHED FOR THE ATEN BY A BINDING DIRECTOR, a virtuous Black woman.

Fact 6

Redemption: A Real-life Scenario

A man kidnaps a baby. He calls the father to demand that he pays $5,000.00 before he will release the baby back to the parents. The demanded price is called a "Ransom." When the ransom is paid in full and the baby released that is considered "Redemption." We are kidnapped victims. Jehovah demands a "Ransom" from The Aten. The "Ransom Price" is the life of The Son of God/Pharaoh. The Pharaoh comes and dies by shedding His precious Divine Blood. The Ransom is paid…BUT JEHOVAH THE GOD OF MISCHIEF DOES NOT RELEASE US!

This is a breech…An "Impassable Interval." The Impassable Interval is an "Uncompromising Position" on "Chattel Slavery," which is considered "a Mystery Between the Two Horizons."

To "Redeem" His Son, The Aten must "Return" to engage in "War." This is considered "A Second Coming."

The Second Coming is called "Secundines." The Secundines is a time of War that will occur during "Horus the Winter," or "Winter Solstice;" and will be spiritually fought by the Egyptian Godhead. To participate in your own "Redemption," you have to OBEY AND FORGET NOT: Deuteronomy 7:25 and 16:12; Isaiah 30:22.

See "Word Study" pages 80 – 86.

The Power of Writing Down My Thoughts (Test Yourself Journaling Page)

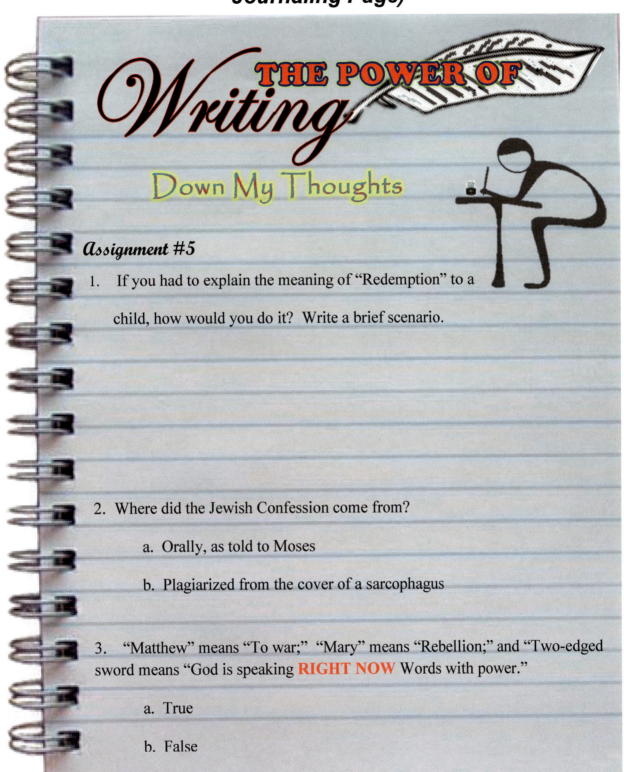

Assignment #5

1. If you had to explain the meaning of "Redemption" to a child, how would you do it? Write a brief scenario.

2. Where did the Jewish Confession come from?

    a. Orally, as told to Moses

    b. Plagiarized from the cover of a sarcophagus

3. "Matthew" means "To war;" "Mary" means "Rebellion;" and "Two-edged sword means "God is speaking **RIGHT NOW** Words with power."

    a. True

    b. False

The Power of Writing Down My Thoughts (Test Yourself Journaling Page)

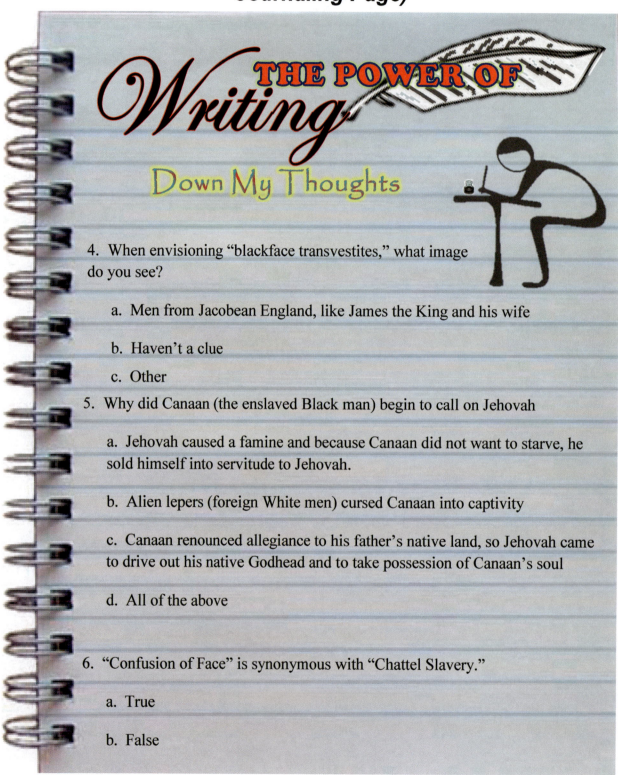

4. When envisioning "blackface transvestites," what image do you see?

   a. Men from Jacobean England, like James the King and his wife

   b. Haven't a clue

   c. Other

5. Why did Canaan (the enslaved Black man) begin to call on Jehovah

   a. Jehovah caused a famine and because Canaan did not want to starve, he sold himself into servitude to Jehovah.

   b. Alien lepers (foreign White men) cursed Canaan into captivity

   c. Canaan renounced allegiance to his father's native land, so Jehovah came to drive out his native Godhead and to take possession of Canaan's soul

   d. All of the above

6. "Confusion of Face" is synonymous with "Chattel Slavery."

   a. True

   b. False

WORD STUDY

Christ = The Messiah = Impassable Interval = Winter

G5547. Christos (CristoV Christos khris-tos') = from 5548; anointed, i.e. **the Messiah,** an epithet of Jesus:--Christ.   See Greek 5548

   5548. chrio (criw chrio khree'-o) = probably akin to 5530 through the idea of contact; to smear or rub with oil, i.e. (by implication) to consecrate to an office or religious service:--anoint.   See Greek 5530

   5530. chraomai (craomai chraomai khrah'-om-ahee) = middle voice of a primary verb (perhaps rather from 5495, to handle); to furnish what is needed; (give an oracle, "graze" (touch slightly), light upon, etc.), i.e. (by implication) to employ or (by extension) to act towards one in a given manner:--entreat, use. Compare 5531; 5534.

   5495. cheir (ceir cheir khire) = perhaps from the base of **5494** in the sense of its congener the base of **5490** (through the idea of hollowness for grasping); the hand (literally or figuratively (power); especially (by Hebraism) a means or instrument):--hand.   See Greek 5494.   See Greek 5490

   5490. chasma (casma chasma khas'-mah) = from a form of an obsolete primary chao (to "gape" or "yawn"); a "chasm" or vacancy **(impassable interval)**:--gulf.

   5494. cheimon (ceimwn cheimon khi-mone') = from a derivative of cheo (to pour; akin to the base of 5490 through the idea of a channel), meaning a storm (as pouring rain); by implication, the rainy season, i.e. winter:--tempest, foul weather, **winter**.

The Lord God Alpha Khen Omega, as dictated to Angela Powell

WORD STUDY

Impassable:

(Hiero Dict) **Impassable** = shta-t: ∞%,",^^",°^ thing rare, curious ; plur. mystery, difficult thing, something hidden, somee X X TfT' C3ED D o^o , IV, 345, 900, mysteries, difficulties; (J -wwva "kv '^j Rec 15, 179, **impassable valleys**; \ U. 207, OS secret ; I I LJSU I ^ w rrvn ^, mysteries of the two horizons ; 3 (^s>- %^ 1 1 1 hidden of forms ; those whose seats are hidden ^, those whose arms are hidden ; II S\I, the god of the hidden soul ; czszi D §., Rec. 26, 231, OZD T^. Litanie 37, ™^| ^ ^ » ^ ^^^ ^^ ~J of invisible body ; czsaD ^^flifli- secret properties; ^^s^^^TT invisible form.

(Hiero Dict) **Impassable** = nti sesh: ^^, ^^^ **intransient**, ァ^^^^ impassable.

in·tran·si·gent also **in·tran·si·geant** (ĭn-trăn′sə-jənt, -zə-) *adjective*
Refusing to moderate a position, especially an extreme position; uncompromising.

Intransi(-g)ent

Indo-European Root

ag- Important derivatives are: *act, agent, agile, ambiguous, essay, exact, navigate,* and *agony.*

To drive, draw, move. **1.** ACT, AGENDUM, AGENT, AGILE, AGITATE; (ALLEGE), AMBAGE, AMBIGUOUS, (ASSAY), (CACHE), COAGULUM, COGENT, ESSAY, EXACT, (EXAMINE), (EXIGENT), FUMIGATE, FUSTIGATE, **INTRANSIGENT**, LEVIGATE, LITIGATE, NAVIGATE, OBJURGATE, PRODIGALITY, RETROACTIVE, SQUAT, TRANSACT, VARIEGATE, from Latin *agere*, to do, act, drive, conduct, lead, weigh. **2.** -AGOGUE, AGONY; ANAGOGE, (ANTAGONIZE), CHORAGUS, DEMAGOGUE, EPACT, GLUCAGON, HYPNAGOGIC, MYSTAGOGUE, PEDAGOGUE, PROTAGONIST, STRATAGEM, SYNAGOGUE, from Greek *agein*, to drive, lead, weigh. **3.** Suffixed form **ag-to-*. AMBASSADOR, EMBASSAGE, (EMBASSY), from Latin *ambactus*, servant, from Celtic **amb(i)-ag-to-*, "one who goes around" (**ambi*, around; see **ambhi**). **4.** Suffixed form **ag-ti-*, whence adjective **ag-ty-o-*, "weighty." AXIOM; AXIOLOGY, CHRONAXIE, from Greek *axios*, worth, worthy, of like value, weighing as much. **5.** Possibly suffixed form **ag-ro-*, driving, pursuing, grabbing. PELLAGRA, PODAGRA, from Greek *agra*, a seizing. [Pokorny aĝ- 4.] Derivative **agro-**.

Indo-European Root

agro-

agro-. Important derivatives are: *acre, pilgrim,* and *agro-*.

Field. Probably a derivative of **ag-**, "to drive" {(<"place to which cattle/{chattel slavery} is driven")}. **1.** ACRE, from Old English *æcer*, field, acre, from Germanic **akraz*. **2.** AGRARIAN; AGRICULTURE, PEREGRINE {falcon: *dark-colored bird v/s white dove*}, (PILGRIM), from Latin *ager* (genitive *agrī*), earlier **agros*, district, property, field. **3.** AGRIA, AIR, AGRO-; (AGROSTOLOGY), ONAGER, STAVESACRE, from Greek *agros*, field, and *agrios*, wild. [In Pokorny aĝ- 4.]

> Interval:
>
> (Hiero Dict) Interval = ahai ^100 ®>^ standing still, pause, interval.
>
> (Hiero Dict) Interval = ush   Heruemheb 23, Rev. 1 1, 150, to be empty, to be decayed or destroyed, or ruined, effaced (of an inscription), bald, hairless, to fall out (of the hair), to lack ; >v"I^ deprived, robbed ; Copt. ,' ush - omission, space, interval, a sign ^ used in papyri to mark a lacuna. usII ^°, nothing, emptiness. ush ^^,^^,^P^,©[j w, darkness, night ; Copt. OlfajH. ush '^C3a'^^, "^j '^];^,, pelican (?) ush v\C30-^, Rec. 4, 12 1, to eat; var. ush (=3), to make water. ush ^, to play the harp. cszirzl ush ^C3a^, j_^^. Amen. 26, 13, V VR' ® [i]l > to cry out, to praise, to adore
>
> (Amer. Hert. Dict.) Interval = **rampart** (to prepare to take possession of); bulwark; boulevard; traverse; furnish forefather boat passage, reciprocal; buckle- that which pierces through; few, little, Paul, powerful, lord; journey, travel, wing – that which carries a bird in flight; a bringing forth, offspring; rampart, parent, who assigns one's destiny, pau- {Paul}; viper – live birth, alive; **postpartum, afterbirth, third stage of birth**; (Pokorny #s 810, 817, 818, pere-1, 842)

> **postpartum, afterbirth, third stage of birth = se·cun·dines**
>
> 3 Stages of Birth:
> (1) Consummation: Conception and Implantation;
> (2) Pregnancy: Fetal Development - 3 Stages of 12 and 13 week trimesters; and Deliverance;
> (3) Afterbirth: Placenta Expulsion, Secundines

Secundines

se·cun·dines = The afterbirth (Pokorny #896). The placenta (Pokorny #831):-- Following; that which follows

Pok. 896, sek = Slack, calm; relax; slowly, a little: ESSONITE = It is less hard than true hyacinth; HYACINTH = See: **Revelation 9:17**; G5192, zirk^{c}on = (Pok. #429) ghel-^{2} = To shine: --yellow; gold; GLIDE, KITE, GLEDE=(< "gliding, hovering bird {See Hiero Dict: tchera-t}"); GLIB=slippery = See: **Psalms 35:6**;
[Middle English *secundinas*, from Late Latin *secundīnae*, from *secundus*, following.]

896, Second Coming, coming next: Isis and Nephthys, To destroy {that which pierces through} = { Set }

831, afterbirth = plagiary = kidnapping = net/flap//net: SEE: brooch, buckle {that which pierces through}

{<Also See: (Revelation 2:2) Fibula:-- Brooch = Word Study on Saul/Paul of Tarsus>} at https://youtu.be/ciJ6kzx7qMc.

"That which pierces through" = set = to cut, to pierce

    set n ff^, n '' L-fl, Israel Stele 4, Tombos Stele 11, Rec 30, 220, I ^w—fl, PT^>PSPT^-P=^- r|
to break, to smash, to cleave, ɪ-^ɪ'^'to breach a wall.

    Set t p ci^ Set—the god of evil.

See Video: Saatt ta, (9-1-1) at https://youtu.be/S8xhjjxVg-s

"gliding, hovering bird {See: tchera-t (Hiero Dict)}"

tchera-t = kite, glede

tcher-t <=, U. 572, p. 475, 673. N. 1262, B o A^, T. 381, hawk, falcon, vulture, kite, glede; plur. B^^^. T. 77; Copt. xpe.

Tcher, Tchera-t B, B« jj^oJ, ^1!M—— of Nephthys both of whom were represented as women, cows or birds, i.e., hawks, vultures, etc. **Isis** was the " Great Ancestress," B* (1 (£ ^^^ ^^ "J, and **Nephthys** the " Little Ancestress,"

tcher B fc^, 243, 280, Rec. 32, 78, B* L-cZI, to bring to an end, i.e., to finish, to fashion, to construct, to make an end of, i.e., to destroy.

tcher B^, B h^, Rec. 21, 39 to bandage, to tie up, to envelop; B o>P\j|, M. 426, bandaged, swathed — 'v"^ 1 1 » T. 268, buried; Copt. XuSX.

tcher-t B.^^, oppression, restraint.

tcher-t -^ ^iSa, U. 3, 550, T. 29, 32, P. 6r3, M. 781, N. 179, 1 138, palm of the hand; Copt. TOOT".

tchera-t B fl '^, Rec. 31, 30, hand.

Tcher-t B^,T. 308, the Great Hand heaven {Ezekiel 8:3}; compare the hand [1) ^h '' m in Tuat

Tchera B ()^, Rec 30, 66, a god.

Tchera-t B (1 ^, b.m. 46631, consort of

tchera-t, vulture, kite, glede

tchera, to work, to finish, to complete, to execute, to be complete or finished; []^B[]^^^, L.D. III, 194, 32, finished, i.e., hewn stones.

tchera B L_J1 (J, IV, 660, strong one or thing; ^^(je^, A.Z. .905, -very, very.

Tchera, B n, ^^^- ^^9, iv, 1087, i Et-J wall, fort. {RAMPART}

tcheru B %^, B.D. 172, 17, vulture, kite, glede; Copt. XpG.

Make Sure To Cross Reference With **TEN PLAGUES PLACED ON EGYPT: MURDERING OUR GODHEAD**

The Lord God Alpha Khen Omega, as dictated to Angela Powell

Winter = wed-1^(Pok. 78) = Water; wet. **4.** Nasalized form *we-n-d-. WINTER, from Old English *winter*, winter, from Germanic *wintruz, winter, "wet season."

wê-r-. An important derivative is: *urine*. {Interval/ush/To make water/SECUNDINES}
Contracted from *weǝ-r-. Water, liquid, milk. Related to **euǝ-dh-ŗ**. Suffixed zero-grade form *ūr-īnā-. URINE, from Latin *ūrīna*, urine. [In Pokorny 9. au(e)- 78.]

eue-dh-R. Derivatives are: *udder,* and *exuberant*.

Udder. Related to **wê-r-**. **1.** Suffixed zero-grade form *ūdh-ŗ. UDDER, from Old English *ūder*, udder, from Germanic *ūdr-. **2.** Suffixed o-grade form *oudh-ŗ. (EXUBERANT), EXUBERATE, from Latin adjective *ūber*, fertile, derived from *ūber*, "breast." [Pokorny ēudh- 347.]

Pok. 347, euk-. To become accustomed. a. suffixed (feminine) from *uk-sor- in Latin uxor, wife (< "she who gets accustomed to the new household" after patri-local marriage): UXORIOUS, UXORICIDE; b. to understand, "get accustomed to"…TWIG²

Pok. 347, eus-. **To burn.** (1.) UREDO, ADUST, BUST¹, COMBUST (2.) To burn, SEE **bhreu**- BROIL¹ (3.) ASHES, EMBER

Pok. 143, **bhreu-²**. Important derivatives are: *brew, ferment,…*
To boil, bubble, **effervesce** **{Javan; Japheth),** burn; with derivatives referring to cooking and brewing.

2779. choreph (Prx choreph kho'-ref) from 2778; properly, the crop gathered, i.e. (by implication) the autumn (and winter) season; figuratively, ripeness of age:--cold, winter (-house), youth. See Hebrew 2778

2778. charaph (Prx charaph. khaw-raf') a primitive root; to pull off, i.e. (by implication) to expose (as by stripping); specifically, to betroth (as if a surrender); figuratively, to carp at, i.e. defame; denominative (from 2779) to spend the winter:-- betroth, blaspheme, defy, jeopard, rail, reproach, upbraid. See Hebrew 2779

Hieroglyphic Dictionary

nen = the winter solstice.

Nekhekh ww, """ """ f"""" ᵒⁿ∧ ᵐ∧ᵐ ᴡᴡ the winter sun.

Nekhekh ww, """ """ f"""" ᵒⁿ∧ ᵐ∧ᵐ ᴡᴡ the sun as an old man, the winter sun. (See File: Winter Sun Nekhekh)

Nekhekh o Thes. 430, a form of Rā, the autumn sun.

Rā sherà G^^(j4,,0^^j , the little sun, i.e., the winter sun.

Horus, the Winter  (See: Page 99), 2015 Winter Healing

Mes·si·ah

Mes·si·ah (mĭ-sī′ə) *noun*
1. Also **Mes·si·as** (mĭ-sī′əs). The anticipated deliverer and king of the Jews.
2. Also **Messias**. Jesus.
3. **messiah.** A leader who is regarded as or professes to be a savior or liberator.
[Middle English *Messias, Messie*, from Old French *Messie*, from Late Latin *Messīās*, from Greek, from Aramaic *měšîḥâ* and or Hebrew *māšăḥ*, the anointed, messiah.]

(.wav) *Māšăḥ* sounds like **Ma·sai** (mä-sī′, mä′sī) *noun plural* **Ma·sais**

sefi P *^O, P '^-^ (j[j 0, unguent, scented oil, an anointed person.
sefi = sword, knife
sefi = to be young, babe, child, a title of the rising sun.
sfa "~~ to strain, to purify; AA/\AAA J » AAAAAA see sefi.
Sefi-peri-em-Hesher, etc. B D. 164, 8, a title of the Sun-god
    baq =
    nen = tT, to smear, to anoint
        Nen,;;,u. 537.^4:1.3:1, B.D. (Saite) 64, 11, the Sky-god.
    nen = the winter solstice.
nen AAAAAA (t-i. 1 1 ^=^» •L-|.*=|» O, salve, ointment. W AAAAAA h rt^-.-V viAAAA /^^ be weary, to be tired, to be helpless, to be in- active, to be inert, to be lazy, to do nothing, to rest, to be sluggish.
        nen 11 J r I, Koller Pap. 4, 8, w indolence; -j-}-^, Rec. 6, 7.
        nen 1 1 c~&^ 'f^ t'f'^ the time of inactivity, the TT *'night.
    (see: Hieroglyphic Dict. for remaining "nen" words.)

610. 'acuwk (Kwoa 'acuwk aw-sook') = from 5480; anointed, i.e. an oil-flask:--pot. See Hebrew 5480. {used only once in 2Kings 4:2}

    5480. cuwk (Kwo cuwk sook) = a primitive root; properly, to smear over (with oil), i.e. anoint:--anoint (self), X at all.

2 Kings 4:2 And Elisha said unto her, What shall I do for thee? tell me, what hast thou in the house? And she said, Thine handmaid hath not any thing in the house, save a pot/anointed (610, 'acuwk) of oil (8080, shaman, a primitive root; to shine/grease/To shine{[Pokorny] ghel–², gold, gliding hovering bird **<Isis and Nephthys>**, etc.}, i.e. (by analogy) be (causatively, make) oily or gross:--become (make, wax) fat..) {used in De 32:15, Ne 9:25, Isa 6:10, and Jer 5:28}; to shine/{[Pokorny] deiw–[183] and de–[183], sky, heaven, god, Tuesday, July, Zeus, Jupiter = **To Bind; RACHEL/Lod/Nativity**}.

Impassable Interval Message

Make Sure To Cross Reference With **TEN PLAGUES PLACED ON EGYPT: MURDERING OUR GODHEAD**

Impassable Interval: Message

A rare thing, a mystery of the two horizons; intransigent = uncompromising position; Falcon, Chattel Slavery… Standing still = SOLSTICE, Rampart = To prepare to take possession of.

3-Stages of Birth

1. Consummation: Conception and Implantion
2. Pregnancy: Fetal Development
3. Secundines = Second Coming = Isis and Nephthys, Winter Solstice, Horus the Winter

Bind Rachel, Jacob
Burn Javan. Jehovah the God of mischief…

The Lord God Alpha Khen Omega, as dictated to Angela Powell

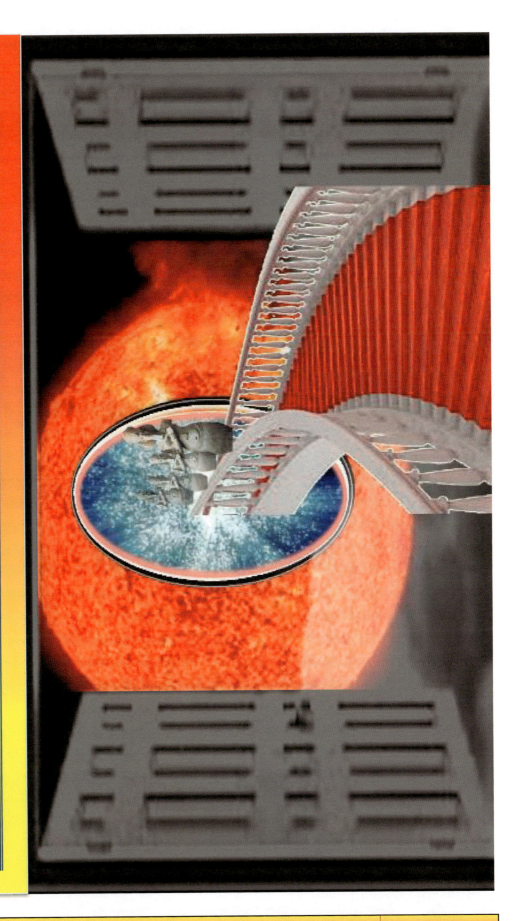

(Revelation 11:19) - And the temple of God was opened in heaven, and there was seen in his temple the ark of his testament: and there were lightnings, and voices, and thunderings, and an earthquake, and great hail.

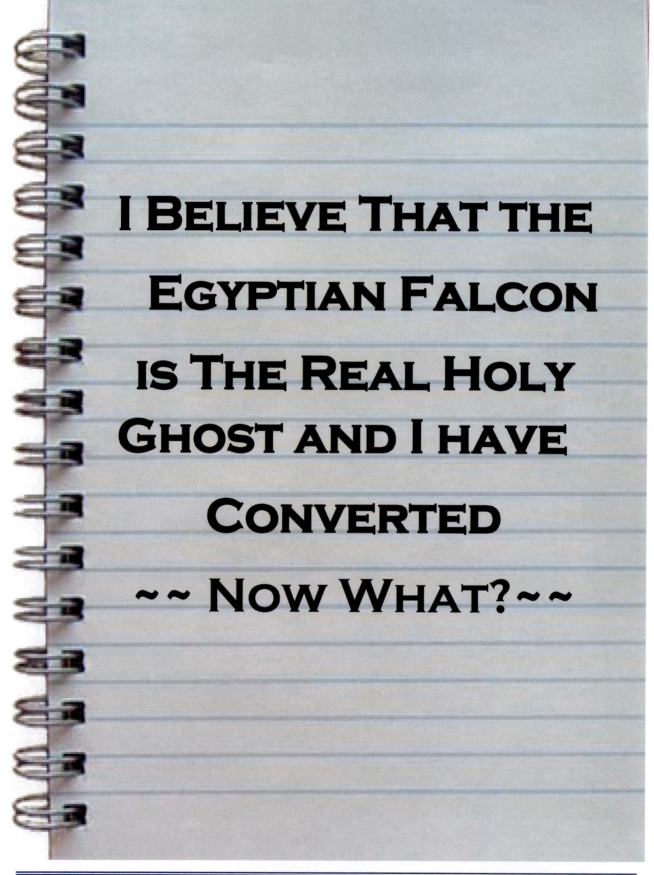

The Lord God Alpha Khen Omega, as dictated to Angela Powell

This is You!
You Are A Spiritual Person Under Amen Covenant of Life; and You Are Now Ready To Stand On
The Sea of Glass Clear As Crystal

For Visual Tutorials Visit: AlphaKhenOmegaNews on YouTube.com

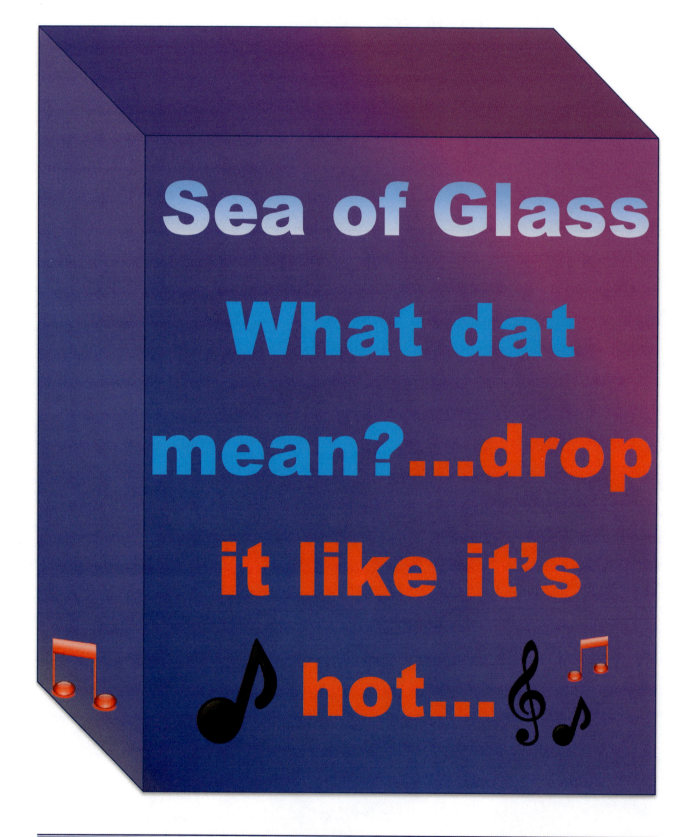

The Lord God Alpha Khen Omega, as dictated to Angela Powell

Revelation 15:1 - 5 - And I saw another sign in heaven, great and marvellous, seven angels having the seven last plagues; for in them is filled up the wrath of God. And I saw as it were a sea of glass mingled with fire: and them that had gotten the victory over the beast, and over his image, and over his mark, and over the number of his name, stand on the sea of glass, having the harps of God. And they sing the song of Moses the servant of God, and the song of the Lamb, saying, Great and marvellous are thy works, Lord God Almighty; just and true are thy ways, thou King of saints. Who shall not fear thee, O Lord, and glorify thy name? for thou only art holy: for all nations shall come and worship before thee; for thy judgments are made manifest. And after that I looked, and, behold, the temple of the tabernacle of the testimony in heaven was opened:

Revelation 15:1 - 4

and them that had gotten the victory over the beast, and over his image, and over his mark, and over the number of his name, stand on the sea of glass, having the harps of God.

How Do I Get The Victory

The Lord Our God do not wish to overwhelm you in one sitting with too much meat! To Get further instructions on getting the VICTORY, go to www.YouTube.com and search for my videos call: Revelation 15:2 Sea of Glass, A Love Song To The Black Man; and No Other Gods Before Me.

Song of The Lamb (Conclusion of the Love Song)
(Need More Time To Read: Remember To PAUSE)

The Love Song of Revelation 15:1-4 is called a sea of glass mingled with fire because it is a pun. Pun means word play. The word 'sea' plays on the word 'salt'. 'Salt' plays on the word 'slavery.' 'Slavery' plays on the words "Salvation," and "saints." The enslaved are the saints and holy seed of Ham who must get the victory over the Beast, over his image, and over his mark, and over the number of his name. When they do, they stand on a sea of glass. The word "glass," means "ankh, mirror, your life." It is also a pun meaning to be 'transparent' like so much 'rain' that it is comparable to a 'sea.' The 'sea' is mingled with 'fire' because the etymological root for "pun" is "peuk-," which means "to prick." "Peuk-" is assigned Pokorny number 828, which also means "pur-." The definition for "pur-" is fire. The primary Song of The Lamb is "And I, if I be lifted up, will draw all men unto Me." "Lamb" by coincident or *divine providence* is "nasa," which means "To lift up." "Nasa" evolves into NASA. "NASAq" means "to catch 'fire.'" NASA's rockets catch fire and lift up. As one redeemed from slavery, you must ensure that you are not "lifted up" and "enslaved" on Mars. How do you keep from being enslaved again? Get VICTORY over the Beast…over his image…over his mark…and over the number of his name.

How do I get the VICTORY?

Make Sure To Cross Reference With **Ten Plagues Placed On Egypt: Murdering Our Godhead**

Blessed Winter So(-ⁿ)l(-tice)
Tuesday
22 December 2015
04:49
~~ DON'T MISS IT ! ~~

REMEMBER AND FORGET NOT

The graven images of their gods shall ye burn with fire; (Deuteronomy 7:25)

And thou shalt remember that thou wast a bondman in *the land of Anguish*: and thou shalt observe and do these statutes: (Deuteronomy 16:12)

thou shalt cast away as a menstruous cloth *the covenant embedded within your Adversary's money*; thou shalt say unto it, Get thee hence. (Isaiah 30:22)

Ask Me, your God "To weigh those who enslave you."

~~The Aten, and his assistant, Lazarus, made the sun stand still when Lazarus was given… and received …the gift of life~~

"Sun stand still" means "Sun Stop;" this means "solstice."

The Winter Solstice shall grace us in a few days. The "Impassable Interval" or "great gulf fix" happens during "nen:" that is to say the Winter Solstice. To obtain your gift of life and life more abundantly, at 04:49 on 22 December 2015, sound the trumpet and make a burning of the White Dove and let Horus the Winter begin His great work of liberating you, the Redeemed, from bondage.

Make Sure To Cross Reference With TEN PLAGUES PLACED ON EGYPT: MURDERING OUR GODHEAD

The Lord God Alpha Khen Omega, as dictated to Angela Powell

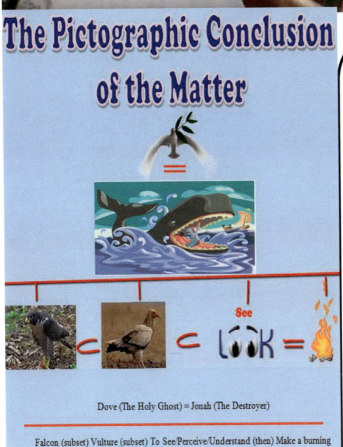

Mystery of the Pictograph

Once you see and seeing believe, and hear and hearing understand that the pictograph means: "Dove=Falcon=Vulture= To See and Understand= Then make a BURNING!"— You need to OBEY.

What are you to BURN?

The Scripture of Truth says:' BURN the images of their Gods."

Your Word Study; "**Effervesce**" says BURN the images of Javan/Japheth/Jehovah the God of mischief.

Redeemed, sons of God, sons of Ham, Jehovah is your archenemy! To receive life and life more abundantly…you must convert! You cannot convert until you utterly overthrow Jehovah from your mind (medulla oblongata) and from your heart. That is why you need to burn his image…IT IS THE FIRST STEP TOWARDS YOUR SELF-LIBERATION.

Make Sure To Cross Reference With TEN PLAGUES PLACED ON EGYPT: MURDERING OUR GODHEAD

The Lord God Alpha Khen Omega, as dictated to Angela Powell

This is the 3,500-hundred-year old TRUMPET of King Tutankhamen. Military Powers affirm that they sound these trumpets prior to going into WAR. If you are ready to join The Army of The Aten to fight in the WAR OF GOG AND MAGOG, then go to https://youtu.be/M8weQjNGXrQ and sound the TRUMPET and make a silent burning!

Do it Tuesday, 22 December 2015, at 04:49 in the morning, at the start of the Winter Solstice. No one has to witness your act of liberation: it is between you and Me, The Lord God Alpha Khen Omega. On this specific date and time—I Will SEE you and honor your act of obedience.

After you blow the trumpets…
Stand, as it were, with one foot on the sea and one foot on the land…because you now have VICTORY over the Beast…over his image…over his mark…and over the number of his name.

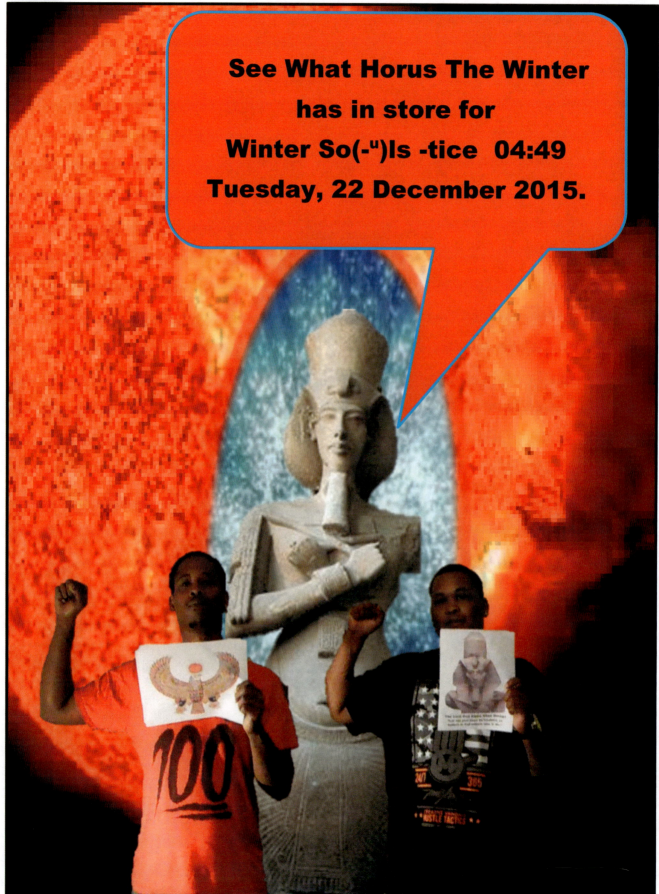

Dear Redeemed,

You are more than likely wondering who am I to ask you to make a burning during the Winter So$^{(-u)}$ls(-tice).

Answer: Nobody!

My assignment from The Lord God Alpha Khen Omega is to write down the lessons that He teaches me during the RIGHT-NOW-time in which He teaches it to me. You are reading a RIGHT NOW Word; it is NOT a preconceived script. Granted, I made a video on 11 July 2014, containing this title; but in it, even though I made a burning, I made no request of you to make a burning. It is God Who is RIGHT NOW saying to you—just like He says to me—if you believe...do a work! Faith without works is dead (James, Chapter 2).

The moment I began to believe in The Lord God Alpha Khen Omega, I had to do works: (1) Write down dreams and visions. (2) Learn how to research "Words" and "Words" only. (3) Read the entire Bible, over-and-over again. (5) Write out my own understanding of each Book. But, the most important of these works is: (6) OBEY! I have to obey those words that SPEAK LOUDLY AND CLEARLY what must need be done.

Having eyes to see and seeing perceive, you now know the definition for each word in our word study, i.e.: Effervesce = TO BURN. Either you choose to OBEY or DISOBEY. Either you choose to BELIEVE or call The Lord God Alpha Khen Omega a liar and NOT believe. Your choice is always up to you!

I am not advocating the hatred of, nor the harming of, nor the killing of any man, woman, nor child. I ask that you use your Holy Ghost Power—your Black power—to reestablish a love of our native African Godhead, "Re-Harakhti-in-His-name-Shu-who-is Aten." The Aten IS NOT mythology! He is alive! He is here, RIGHT NOW! His Second Coming is going on while you are deliberating on *when is He coming back*!

As for me, I see His face. He commands my steps. I am His servant—not to be confused with slave—because He is not an evil, conniving taskmaster. I am free to choose, like you, to believe what He says and to OBEY or DISobey. I choose to obey—that is why you are able to read His words written by my hand as a willing vessel of The Aten.

As His binding director, I am just one of many, past, present, and future virtuous Black women who have read, and then listened to the readings, and then interpreted the words, and then believed and obeyed the Word up to the point of setting the White supremacy master's idols on fire.

At first, it caused me great mental anguish because, yes—as sad and conflicting as it may be—I loved the race that so evil-entreated my ancestors. In fact, even though it is sickening, I still participate in things appertaining to my enemies' cultures, even their schools and colleges where a White professor taught that Black people are the CURSE OF HAM. I was made to approve or disprove the White man's stance. I ended up praying over the matter, and as a result The Lord God Alpha Khen Omega came into my life to show me that if the evil taskmasters whom I befriend and emulate make it to Mars, they plan to once again enslave Black men, so that we may till the barren grounds of whatever planet they can Rapture us up to.

I was so afraid of their plots that I developed mental illness. I overcome it day-by-day when I burn idolatrous images of the (-ir) Father, Son, and Holy Ghost. It is healing for my enslaved soul, more so than any amount of reparations; more so than marching on the Capitol for rights that only last over night; more so than boycotting Florida or Black Friday. Plus, it solidifies my personal relationship with our native Godhead, Who says, "Have NO other Gods before Me and BURN their images." I choose to obey God.

You do not have to post your act of obedience on YouTube. You do not have to publish it in a book. All you have to do is: Think about the horrors…the evil…the injustice of slavery—think about why there has never been any reconciliation wherein a man was punished for crimes against our humanity. Once you think about it, you should desire justice…and the only way to get justice is to turn to God. Ask The Lord yOur God to weigh the hearts of the oppressors. Then recall to mind, He said, "As in Heaven so in the Earth and as in Earth so in Heaven." As The Lord yOur God weighs the White supremacy masters' hearts, He equips you to do the same works as He does it.

Once you see that the White man cannot apologize, neither repent, neither love a Black God Who is The Creator and Maker of the Heavens, the Earth, the seas and all that therein is~~ once you see that he cannot love The Lord God Alpha Khen Omega-in-His human form known as Pharaoh Akhenaton~~ doing God's work is easy because

Make Sure To Cross Reference With **TEN PLAGUES PLACED ON EGYPT: MURDERING OUR GODHEAD**

BURNING the idolatrous images of the White masters' Gods of mischief is holy work that ushers in The Kingdom of The Lord God Alpha Khen Omega.

If you choose to burn the idols, do it in secret to The Lord God Alpha Khen Omega. He sees and hears your secrets. You do not have to commit violence to any man. God, Himself, does the avenging and brings in the JUSTICE. All you have to do is obey His Word. If you want God to open up the windows of Heaven and pour out the blessings of recompense and punishment against the oppressors, then at 04:49 on Tuesday, 22 December 2015, sound King Tutankhamen's WAR TRUMPETS and make a burning. If you miss the 2015 Winter Solstice, *I think* that the commandment of The Lord God Alpha Khen Omega will still be in effect for a few upcoming Winter Solstices. Winter Solstices only last a few minutes each year. Their exact times are listed according to the Coordinated Universal Time (UTC), which can be accessed on-line or any good almanac.

Here is the link to help you get started: King Tutankhamen's Trumpets To Be Sounded During Winter Solstice 2015 at
https://www.youtube.com/edit?o=U&video_id=M8weQjNGXrQ

I do not hate White people...*sorry, I just don't!* I am a non-violent lover of all mankind. Therefore, I do not want war! But, hey, The War of Gog and Magog is already written and must be fulfilled. You and I will of a necessity join a spiritual army-- whether Jehovah the God of mischief...or, The Aten the God of righteousness with healing in His wings...we are destined to join~~ or be spewed out of The Mouth of God (Revelation 3:16)!

Picture that verse! The Bible so kindly calls it "spued out," but *Strong's Concordance* calls it for what it is...A Lukewarm Person Is An Upset Stomach To God and He Must Vomit You Out Of His Mouth/Kingdom To Relieve His Anguish/Egyptian Soul.

Throughout this Book of Witness, The Lord God Alpha Khen Omega speaks RIGHT NOW words that let us know He is here, waiting for us to obey Him, and to convert and be healed of our Curse of Captivity. On the next few pages, I will show you how I use the concordance to help me interpret and translate God's Word; so that you, too, may come on board and hear God speak. After you learn to translate, it could be that God will lift you up...right into The Sun...through dreams and visions...so that you can SEE His Face, and Believe on Him, and serve Him with *your* unique God-given gifts and talents.

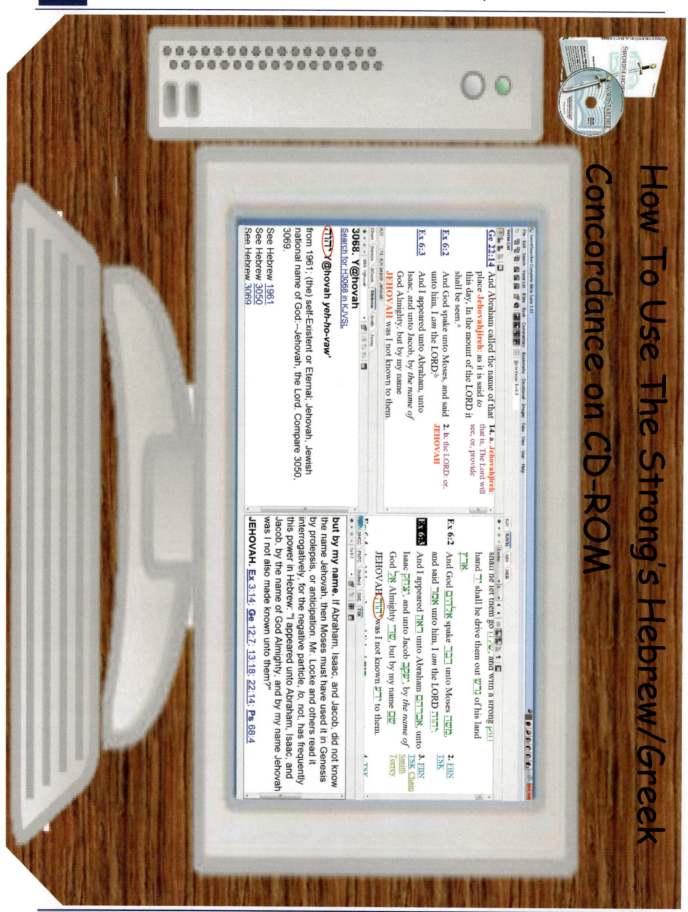

How To Use The Strong's Hebrew/Greek Concordance on CD-ROM

Make Sure To Cross Reference With TEN PLAGUES PLACED ON EGYPT: MURDERING OUR GODHEAD

The Lord God Alpha Khen Omega, as dictated to Angela Powell

INSTRUCTIONS:

➢ On the adjacent page is an image on my computer screen.

➢ It is displaying *The Sword Searchers* program on CD-ROM.

➢ To use the program, I type the name "Jehovah," in the program's "Search" box.

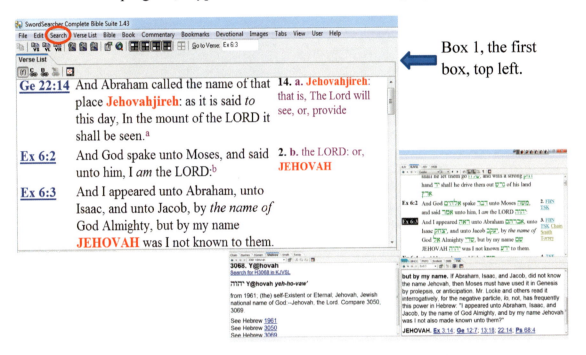

Box 1, the first box, top left.

➢ Every Scripture with the name "Jehovah" will display in "Box 1," the first box, top left.

   o For this study, I chose Exodus 6:3, the Scripture where God tells Abraham that the ancient people did not know him by the name of JEHOVAH. (Jehovah came later, in your timeframe, circa AD 1530-1611.)

- Next, I move on to "Box 2," the box located top right.

    o It displays the actual verse Exodus 6:3 that was chosen in "Box 1," along with its Hebrew (Old Testament) *(or Greek for New Testament)* definitions.

Box 2, the box located, top right. →

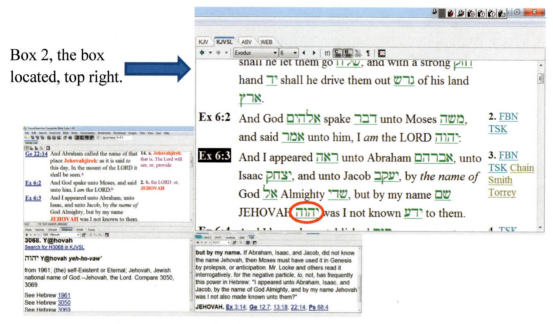

    o The green underlined characters are Hebrew words that come from *Strong's Concordance*, which is linked to *Sword Searchers* kjv Bible. It is easier and faster to use the Concordance on CD-ROM than it is to use the hardbound edition.

    o The kjv Bible only uses the actual name "Jehovah" a total of seven times. When referencing God, the kjv uses the terms "God," "Lord," and "Lord God."

    o When I hover my mouse on the green character for Jehovah, the definition displays in "Box 3."

- In "Box 3," lower left, the Hebraic definition for the name "Jehovah" displays. It is assigned the number H3068. "H" stands for Hebrew; "G" stands for Greek.

- "Box 4," lower right, displays all scholarly commentaries associated with the biblical verse.

- Back to "Box 3." All Hebrew, Aramaic, and Greek words are assigned a number.
  - The number for "JEHOVAH," H3068, reads that it comes from the number H1961. So you are supposed to go to the "Search" box and type in H1961. This will display the root word for the name Jehovah. It will also tell you which action to take next.

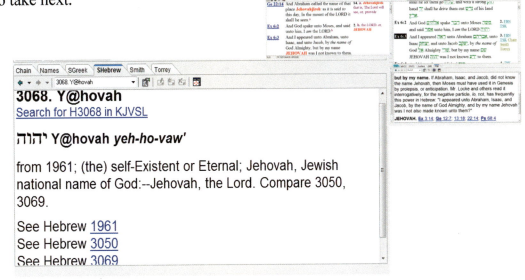

- The definition for the name "Jehovah," which is number H3068, Y@hovah, reads: From 1961; (the) self-Existent or Eternal; Jehovah, Jewish national name of God:--Jehovah, the Lord. Compare 3050, 3069.

- The definition for H1961 reads: A primitive root (compare 1933); to exist, i.e. be or become, come to pass (always emphatic, and not a mere copula or auxiliary):--beacon, X altogether, be(-come), accomplished, committed, like), break, cause, come (to pass), do, faint, fall, + follow, happen, X have, last, pertain, quit (one-)self, require, X use.
  See Hebrew 1933.

- To shorten the process, once you go through all the instructions and follow all the links to see this number or that number you end up with a word study chart that should look like this:

WORD STUDY

Jehovah = God of mischief

Jehovah	Jah + hovah = God of mischief
H3068. Y@hovah - from 1961; (the) self- Existent or Eternal; Jehovah, Jewish national name of God:--Jehovah, the Lord. See Hebrew 1961; See H3050; See H3069	H3050. Yahh - contraction for **3068**, and meaning the same; Jah, the sacred name: --**Jah,** the Lord, most vehement. See Hebrew 3068
H1961. hayah - a primitive root; to exist, i.e. be or become, come to pass. See Hebrew 1933	+
H1933. hava¹ a primitive root; **to breathe**. See H183; See H1961	H1943. **hovah** - another form for 1942; ruin:-- **mischief**
H183. 'avah - a primitive root; to wish for:--covet	**H1942. havvah** - from 1933 (in the sense of eagerly Coveting and rushing upon; by implication, of falling); desire; also ruin:-- calamity, iniquity, **mischief,** mischievous (thing), naughtiness, noisome, perverse thing, substance, **very wickedness.** See Hebrew 1933.
H3050. Yahh - contraction for **3068**, and meaning the same; Jah, the sacred name:--Jah, the Lord, most vehement. See Hebrew 3068	H1933. hava'- a primitive root; To Breath. See Hebrew 183; See Hebrew
	"To Breath" = Terah, the father of Abraham

Taken from *Strong's Hebrew/Greek Concordance*

Answer Key

Assignment #2

Pharaoh Akhenaton introduces Himself as The Lord God Alpha Khen Omega. Pharaoh Akhenaton is The Son of The Aten. He is here speaking RIGHT NOW Words to the Redeemed, whom He calls Team Atenites. He wants them to convert and be healed from their Curse of Captivity. Using a pictograph, He wants His team to answer His question about Who or What is The Holy Ghost; and He asks them should The Holy Ghost be portray as a "White Dove?" or, as an ancient "Egyptian Falcon?"

A "Word Study" is given to help us define the word "Dove." It means "Destroyer." Dove is also a subset of the word "Falcon." "Falcon" is a subset of the word "Vulture." "Vulture" is a subset of a word meaning: "To See" and "To Burn."

After learning that The Holy Ghost should be portrayed as a "Falcon," Pharaoh Akhenaton tackles the subject of Who is The Holy Ghost. He is first introduced in the New Testament where it is written of Him: "Before Mary and Joseph came together, Mary was found with child of The Holy Ghost." Therefore, Team Atenites are sent to read and comprehend Matthew 1:1 – 25, with special emphasis on Matthew 1:18, which is considered a "MYSTERY."

Assignment #3

The Aten is The Father. He is the Sun in Heaven. Using a director, whom He teaches His Words via DNA/RNA transcription, and through dreams and visions, He speaks to His Team Atenites. He tells them Pharaoh Akhenaton is His Son, and their Deliverer. This is a book about Their Second Coming, which is going on RIGHT NOW. Using words that are already written in the Bible, His real-life story is being rewritten with current definitions that disclose Mysteries for us to understand what is happening, today. The Aten's "coronal ejections" are signs of war being fought by Pharaoh Akhenaton-in-His-new name-The Lord God Alpha Khen Omega. He is here to redeem those who are enslaved.

Assignment #4

Pharaoh Akhenaton introduces Himself as The Lord God Alpha Khen Omega. He is The Son of The Aten. He is here speaking RIGHT NOW Words to the Redeemed, whom He calls Team Atenites. He wants us to convert and be healed from our Curse of Captivity that Noah damned us to. Using a pictograph, He wants His team to solve a mystery of Who or What is The Holy Ghost; and He asks should The Holy Ghost be portray as a "White Dove?" or, and ancient "Egyptian Falcon?"

"Dove" means "Destroyer." "Dove" is also a subset of the word "Falcon." "Falcon" is a subset of the word "Vulture." "Vulture" is a subset of a word meaning: "To See" and "To Burn" idolatrous images of false-Gods.

Our true Godhead is The Father (The Aten--the Sun of righteousness with healing in His wings), and The Son (Pharaoh Akhenaton), and The Holy Ghost (portrayed as the ancient Egyptian Falcon). This is a book about Their Second Coming, which is going on RIGHT NOW with The Aten's "coronal ejections" being signs of war fought by Pharaoh Akhenaton. They are here to redeem those of us who are enslaved and to keep us from going into a third period of bondage. But, first we must understand the Mystery of the Virgin Birth.

The Book of Matthew tells us about the birth of The Son of God, who was conceived of a virgin and begotten of The Holy Ghost. The Hebrew word for "Birth" is "Nativity." "Nativity" comes from the word "Lod."

"Lod" is a mystery. "Lod" means both "Ludim" and "Lud."

If you take the pathway to the nativity of "Lud," it leads you into the family of Abraham, Isaac, and Jacob. They high jacked the nativity story from "Ludim." "Ludim" is representative of "Egypt." For a punishment for their sins against The Aten, He tells them the Day of their Judgement is RIGHT NOW. The Aten shows us through words and pictures that He is binding Rachel, Jacob, Dan, and the whole klan of Shem and Japheth. The Aten also tells us (with words and pictures that He is taking away the idolatrous images of both "The White Dove" and "The White Knight/Savior," being called Jesus Christ). The patriarchs of the Bible consorted with "Talismans," "Gods of mischief," and "Apollyon, the Destroyer" to try to usurp the Kingdom of God. Apollyon and Jehovah the God of mischief are plotting to enslave the Redeemed on Mars, and they are rallying their heirs (the seed of Shem and Japheth-- who are the image and sons of Jehovah/Zeus) to the War of Gog and Magog.

The Aten is here to destroy them with fire from Heaven/The Sun. His enemies shall not win. The captivity that they have plotted for us shall reverse and bind their own necks, and they shall find themselves hanging from the gallows like Haman. Nothing is left for them in this world…but weeping and gnashing of teeth.

Picture Credits:

Gold Medalist, Tommie Smith, "Black Power Salute"

Some of the pictures and gifs within this publication were taken from:

www.google.com (I only used gifs labeled with "permission to reuse" from their image files).

www.wikipedia.com (Creative Commons)

Microsoft Word's Clipart

2015 — Will The Real Holy Ghost Please Stand Up

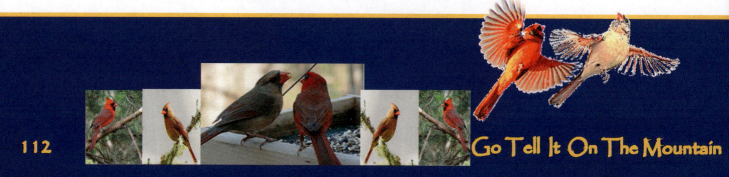

Go Tell It On The Mountain

Made in the USA
Charleston, SC
03 June 2016